First World War
and Army of Occupation
War Diary
France, Belgium and Germany

60 DIVISION
181 Infantry Brigade
London Regiment
2/21 Battalion
1 November 1915 - 30 May 1916

WO95/3032/3

The Naval & Military Press Ltd
www.nmarchive.com
Published in association with The National Archives

Published by

The Naval & Military Press Ltd

Unit 10 Ridgewood Industrial Park,

Uckfield, East Sussex,

TN22 5QE England

Tel: +44 (0) 1825 749494

www.naval-military-press.com

www.nmarchive.com

This diary has been reprinted in facsimile from the original. Any imperfections are inevitably reproduced and the quality may fall short of modern type and cartographic standards.

© Crown Copyright
Images reproduced by permission of The National Archives, London, England, 2015.

Contents

Document type	Place/Title	Date From	Date To
Heading	WO95/3032/3		
Heading	60th Division 181st Infy Bde 2-21st Bn London Regt 1915 Oct-1916 Nov		
Heading	War Diary of the 2/21st Battalion The London Regt. From 1st 30th June 1916		
War Diary	Sutton Veny	01/06/1916	24/06/1916
War Diary	Warminster	24/06/1916	24/06/1916
War Diary	Sutton Veny	24/06/1916	24/06/1916
War Diary	Warminster	24/06/1916	24/06/1916
War Diary	Southampton	24/06/1916	24/06/1916
War Diary	Havre	25/06/1916	26/06/1916
War Diary	Pt Houvin	26/10/1916	26/10/1916
War Diary	St. Pol	26/06/1916	26/06/1916
War Diary	St. Pol	27/06/1916	27/06/1916
War Diary	Pt Houvin	27/06/1916	27/06/1916
War Diary	Ecoivres	27/06/1916	27/06/1916
War Diary	Tinques	28/06/1916	28/06/1916
War Diary	Louez	28/06/1916	30/06/1916
Miscellaneous	2/21st Battalion, The London Regiment Programme Of Training For The Week Commencing 29th May 1916.	27/05/1916	27/05/1916
Miscellaneous	2/21st Battalion The London Regiment Programme Of Training For Week Commencing. 5th June 1916	05/06/1916	05/06/1916
Miscellaneous	2/21st Battalion The London Regiment Programme Of Training For Week Commencing. 12th June 1916	12/06/1916	12/06/1916
Miscellaneous	Battalion Orders No. 3 For 30/6/16 By Lt. Colonel B. Fletcher Commanding 2/21st Battalion, The London Regiment.	30/06/1916	30/06/1916
Miscellaneous	Table Of Moves Of The 2/21st Battalion, The London Regt.		
Heading	War Diary of the 2/21st Battalion The London Regiment. From 1st July 1916 To 31st July 1916.		
War Diary		01/07/1916	02/07/1916
War Diary	Louez	02/07/1916	07/07/1916
War Diary	Maroeuil	08/07/1916	08/07/1916
War Diary	Chelers	09/07/1916	13/07/1916
War Diary	Etrun	14/07/1916	20/07/1916
War Diary	Ecurie	21/07/1916	27/07/1916
War Diary	Ecurie Right Sector	28/07/1916	28/07/1916
War Diary	Etrun	28/07/1916	28/07/1916
War Diary	Right 1 Sector	29/07/1916	31/07/1916
Miscellaneous	Table Of Moves Of 2/21st Battalion, The London Regiment.		
Miscellaneous	Battalion Order No.4 For 8/7/16 By Lt. Col. B. Fletcher Commanding 2/21st Battalion, The London Regiment	07/07/1916	07/07/1916
Operation(al) Order(s)	Operation Order No.2 By Lt. Colonel B. Fletcher	16/07/1916	16/07/1916
Miscellaneous	Instructions		
Heading	War Diary of the 2/21st Battalion London Regiment From 1st To 31st August 1916		
War Diary		01/08/1916	04/08/1916
War Diary	Etrun	04/08/1916	31/08/1916

Heading	War Diary of the 2/21st Battalion London Regiment From 1st To 30th September 1916		
War Diary	In Front Line Trenches	01/09/1916	04/09/1916
War Diary	Etrun	05/09/1916	09/09/1916
War Diary	In Front Line Trenches	10/09/1916	16/09/1916
War Diary	Ecurie	17/09/1916	22/09/1916
War Diary	In Front Line Trenches	23/09/1916	28/09/1916
War Diary	Etrun	29/09/1916	30/09/1916
Heading	War Diary of the 2/21st Battalion, London Regiment From 1/10/16 To 31/10/16		
War Diary	Etrun	01/10/1916	06/10/1916
War Diary	In Front Line Trenches	07/10/1916	10/10/1916
War Diary	Eourie	10/10/1916	25/10/1916
War Diary	Maroeuil	26/10/1916	28/10/1916
War Diary	Izel-Les-Hameau	27/10/1916	27/10/1916
War Diary	Wamin	27/10/1916	28/10/1916
War Diary	Neuvilette	29/10/1916	29/10/1916
War Diary	Autheux	30/09/1916	30/09/1916
Operation(al) Order(s)	2/21st Battalion, The London Regiment Battalion Move Orders No.12 For 4/10/16.	04/10/1916	04/10/1916
Operation(al) Order(s)	2/21st Battalion. The London Regiment. Battalion Move Orders No. 14 For 25/10/16	23/10/1916	23/10/1916
Operation(al) Order(s)	Battalion Orders No. 15 For 26/10/16	25/10/1916	25/10/1916
Operation(al) Order(s)	Battalion Orders No.16 for 27/10/16	26/10/1916	26/10/1916
Operation(al) Order(s)	Battalion Orders No.17 for 28/10/16	27/10/1916	27/10/1916
Operation(al) Order(s)	Battalion Orders No.18 for 29/10/16	28/10/1916	28/10/1916
Operation(al) Order(s)	Battalion Orders No. 20 for 31/10/16	30/10/1916	30/10/1916
Heading	War Diary of the 2/21st Battalion London Regiment From 1/11/16 To 30/11/16		
War Diary	Autheux	01/11/1916	03/11/1916
War Diary	Berneuil	04/11/1916	04/11/1916
War Diary	Villers	05/11/1916	23/11/1916
War Diary	Marseilles	26/11/1916	30/11/1916
Operation(al) Order(s)	Battalion Orders No. 49 For 30/11/16 by Col. F.D. Watney Comdg. 2/21st Battalion, London Regt.	29/11/1916	29/11/1916
Operation(al) Order(s)	Battalion Move Orders No.26 For 23/11/16	22/11/1916	22/11/1916
Operation(al) Order(s)	Battalion Move Orders No.25 For 4/11/16	03/11/1916	03/11/1916
Operation(al) Order(s)	Battalion Move Orders No.24 For 3/11/16	02/11/1916	02/11/1916
Heading	60 Division 181 Brigade 2/21 London Regt. 1915 Oct-1916 May		
War Diary	Hockerill And Neighbourhood Hadham Park Trenching Ground Bishops Stortford And Neighbourhood		
War Diary	Hockerill Camp and Neighbourhood Braintree Dunmow		
War Diary	Braintree Dunmow		
War Diary	Hadham Park		
War Diary	Bishops Stortford Dunmow Coggeshall	01/11/1915	01/11/1915
War Diary	Hockerill	01/11/1915	01/11/1915
War Diary	Great Dunmow	02/11/1915	02/11/1915
War Diary	Coggeshall	03/11/1915	30/11/1915
Heading	War Diary of the 2/21st Battalion, The London Regiment From 1st December 1915 To 31st December 1915.		
War Diary	Coggeshall	01/12/1915	31/12/1915
Miscellaneous	181st Infantry Brigade Tactical Exercise		

Miscellaneous	181st Infantry Brigade Tactical Exercise Battalion Orders By Major B.Fletcher Commanding 2/21st Battalion, The London Regiment	17/12/1915	17/12/1915
Miscellaneous	181st Infantry Brigade	21/12/1915	21/12/1915
Operation(al) Order(s)	181st Brigade Order No.2		
Miscellaneous	Special Order By Major B. Fletcher, Commanding 2/21st Battalion The London Regiment.	25/12/1915	25/12/1915
Miscellaneous	General Idea		
Operation(al) Order(s)	181st Infantry Brigade Order No.1	29/12/1915	29/12/1915
Miscellaneous	181st Infantry Brigade Tactical Exercise 31st December 1915	31/12/1915	31/12/1915
Heading	War Diary of the 2/21st Battn The London Regt January 1st To 31st 1916		
War Diary	Coggeshall	01/06/1916	26/06/1916
War Diary	Sutton Veny	27/06/1916	30/06/1916
Miscellaneous	Programme of Training Snipers.		
Miscellaneous	Battalion Orders By Major B. Fletcher Commanding The 2/21st Battalion, The London Regiment.	07/01/1916	07/01/1916
Miscellaneous	General Idea		
Miscellaneous	Scheme For Night Operations 19/1/16 General Idea	19/01/1916	19/01/1916
Operation(al) Order(s)	181st Infantry Brigade Order 118	12/01/1916	12/01/1916
Miscellaneous	Instructions.		
Miscellaneous	Battalion Orders No.1 By Major. B. Fletcher Commanding 2/21st Battalion London Regiment.	19/01/1916	19/01/1916
Miscellaneous	Notes on Relieving Etc. in Trenches.		
Map	Map		
Miscellaneous	Report On Tactical Scheme At Feering on 19th January 1916 By Capt. And Adjutant A.J. Walter.	20/01/1916	20/01/1916
Heading	War Diary of the 2/21st Battalion London Regiment From 1st To 29th February 1916		
War Diary	Sutton Veny	01/02/1916	29/02/1916
Miscellaneous	Appendix I	27/01/1916	27/01/1916
Miscellaneous	Notes		
Miscellaneous	Extract from 60th (London) Division (T.F.) Orders by Major General E.S. Bulfin, C.V.O., C.B. Commanding.	01/02/1916	01/02/1916
Miscellaneous	Tactical Exercise Held On 17th February 1916		
Miscellaneous	Divisional Exercise	16/02/1916	16/02/1916
Operation(al) Order(s)	60th London Divisional Order No.10	16/02/1916	16/02/1916
Operation(al) Order(s)	181st Brigade Order No.1	15/02/1916	15/02/1916
Miscellaneous	2/21st Battalion, The London Regiment. Programme Of Training For Week Commencing. 17/4/1916	17/04/1916	17/04/1916
Miscellaneous	Officer Commanding 181st Infantry Brigade.	15/02/1916	15/02/1916
Miscellaneous	Precis Of Remarks By G.O.C. 60th (London) Division By Capt And Adj. A.J. Walter.		
Miscellaneous	D.S.T. 1st Line Transport 60th (2/2nd. (London) Division Sutton Veny.	18/02/1916	18/02/1916
Miscellaneous	C.R., S.C., No. 90665/25 (R) Date of Inspection Feb. 21st 1916 60th (London) Division.	21/02/1916	21/02/1916
Heading	War Diary of the 2/21st Battalion London Regt. From 1st To 31st March 1916		
War Diary	Sutton Veny	01/06/1916	30/06/1916
Miscellaneous	2/21st Battalion The London Regiment.	04/03/1916	04/03/1916
Miscellaneous	2/21st Battalion, The London Regiment Trained Men's Programme of Training for Week Commencing.	13/03/1916	13/03/1916
Miscellaneous	2/21st Battalion, The London Regiment Programme Of Training For Week Ending 25th March 1916	18/03/1916	18/03/1916

Miscellaneous	2/21st Battalion, The London Regiment Programme Of Training For Week Commencing 27th March 1916	27/03/1916	27/03/1916
Heading	War Diary of the 2/21st Battalion Loud Regt From 1st To 30th April 1916.		
War Diary	Sutton Veny	01/04/1916	30/04/1916
Miscellaneous	2/21st Battalion, The London Regiment Programme Of Training For Week Commencing 3rd April 1916	03/04/1916	03/04/1916
Miscellaneous	2/21st Battalion, The London Regiment Programme Of Training For Week Commencing 10th April 1916	16/04/1916	16/04/1916
Miscellaneous	2/21st Battalion The London Regiment Programme Of Training For Week Commencing 24/4/16	24/04/1916	24/04/1916
Heading	War Diary of the 2/21st Battalion London Regiment From 1st To 31st May 1916		
War Diary	Sitton Veny	01/05/1916	30/05/1916
Miscellaneous	2/21st Battalion The London Regiment. Programme Of Training For Week Commencing 1st May 1916	30/04/1916	30/04/1916
Miscellaneous	2/21st Battalion The London Regiment. Programme Of Training For Week Commencing 8th May 1916	07/05/1916	07/05/1916
Miscellaneous	2/21st Battalion The London Regiment. Programme Of Training For Week Commencing 10/5/16	13/05/1916	13/05/1916
Miscellaneous	2/21st Battalion The London Regiment. Programme Of Training For Week Commencing 22nd May 1916	21/05/1916	21/05/1916
Miscellaneous	2/21st Battalion The London Regiment. Programme Of Training For Week Commencing 29th May 1916	27/05/1916	27/05/1916

WO 95/3032/3

60TH DIVISION
181ST INFY BDE

2-21ST BN LONDON REGT

~~JUN — NOV 1916~~

1915 OCT — 1916 NOV

Volume 6

Vol I

War Diary
of the
2/21st Battalion The London Regt.
from
1st – 30th June 1916.

Army Form C. 2118.

WAR DIARY
or
INTELLIGENCE SUMMARY.
(Erase heading not required.)

Instructions regarding War Diaries and Intelligence Summaries are contained in F. S. Regs., Part II. and the Staff Manual respectively. Title pages will be prepared in manuscript.

Place	Date	Hour	Summary of Events and Information	Remarks and references to Appendices
SUTTON VENY	1916 June 1st to 4th		Training as per Divisional Programme	See Appendix I
	5th		Arrival of draft of 86 men from 3/5th London Regt (London Rifle Brigade)	
	5th to 11th		Training as per Divisional Programme	See Appendix II
	12th to 18th		Training as per Divisional Programme	See Appendix III
	19th to 23rd		Preparation for service overseas relieving Camp &c	
	21st		Arrival of draft of 13 men from 1/1st 26units Cyclist Battalion	
	24th		Strength of Battalion proceeding overseas 32 Officers 942 Other ranks	

Army Form C. 2118.

WAR DIARY
or
INTELLIGENCE SUMMARY.

(Erase heading not required.) Ref Map France LENS 11 Scale 100,000

Instructions regarding War Diaries and Intelligence Summaries are contained in F. S. Regs., Part II. and the Staff Manual respectively. Title pages will be prepared in manuscript.

Place	Date 1916 June	Hour	Summary of Events and Information	Remarks and references to Appendices
SUTTON VENY	24	8.20 a.m	Headquarters & A & B Companies left for overseas under LT. COL. B. FLETCHER.	
WARMINSTER		9.40	Entrained in 1 train for SOUTHAMPTON	
SUTTON VENY		9.25	C & D Companies left for overseas under MAJOR S. WRIGHT.	
WARMINSTER		10.50	Entrained	
SOUTHAMPTON		12.30 p.m	Arrival of 1st train	
		1.30	" " 2nd "	
		3.45	Battalion, less 4 Officers 195 men transport, embarked under LT. COL. FLETCHER in transport S.S. "La Marguerite"	
		5 p.m	4 Officers 195 men transport, embarked under MAJOR R.A. PUCKLE on transport S.S. "Hunslet".	
HAVRE	25	7.15 a.m	Battalion dis-embarked off "La Marguerite".	
		7.30	Detachment on S.S. Hunslet dis-embarked	
		9.15	Battalion arrived at Docks Rest Camp	
		10 a.m	Detachment " " " "	
	26	4 a.m	Battalion, less 1 Company (D) left camp for GARE DES MERCHANDISES, HAVRE Point No 3 to entrain	

Army Form C. 2118.

WAR DIARY
or
INTELLIGENCE SUMMARY.

(Erase heading not required.) Ref. Map FRANCE LENS 11 Scale 1/100000

Instructions regarding War Diaries and Intelligence Summaries are contained in F. S. Regs., Part II. and the Staff Manual respectively. Title pages will be prepared in manuscript.

Place	Date 1916 June	Hour	Summary of Events and Information	Remarks and references to Appendices
HAVRE.	26	6.30 a.m	D Company under Capt A.J. Walter left camp for tram station to entrain with C & D Batteries 302nd Brigade R.F.A.	
		8 a.m	Battalion, less 1 Company, in 1 train left for St. Pol.	
		9.45 a.m	Train containing D Company re left for Pt. Houvin	
ST. POL.		10.30 p.m	Arrival of Battalion at St. Pol.	
Pt. HOUVIN		11.30 p.m	Arrival of D Company re at Pt. Houvin.	
ST. POL.	27	1.30 a.m	Battalion marched to billets at Ecoivres	
Pt. HOUVIN		2 a.m	D Company " " " "	
ECOIVRES		2.55 a.m	" arrived from detraining station	
		3 a.m	Battalion arrived from station	
		1.30 p.m	Battalion marched to Tinques proceeding by way of Pt. Houvin - Buneville - Ternas.	
TINQUES.		7.30 p.m	Arrived at Tinques, where battalion was billeted.	
	28	6.30 p.m	Battalion marched to Louez by way of Vandelicourt - Savy - Haute-Avesnes - Etrun.	
LOUEZ		11.30 p.m	Arrival at Louez where battalion was billeted. Transport returning to Etrun	

Army Form C. 2118.

WAR DIARY
or
INTELLIGENCE SUMMARY.

Ref. Map FRANCE. LENS 11 Scale 1/100,000

(Erase heading not required.)

Instructions regarding War Diaries and Intelligence Summaries are contained in F. S. Regs., Part II. and the Staff Manual respectively. Title pages will be prepared in manuscript.

Place	Date	Hour	Summary of Events and Information	Remarks and references to Appendices
	1916 June			
LOUEZ	29		Battalion rested in Billets.	
	30		The Battalion being less 287 all ranks, proceed to trenches for instruction with 4th Seaforth Highlanders, 154th Brigade, 51st Division and 9th Royal Scots of the same Brigade.	Appendix IV
			List of Stores of Importance received during the month.	
		3"	Kitchens Travelling	4
		4"	Sgnt Major equipment	
		5"	Grenade Dummies	250
		12"	Bags Sand	200
	"		Carts, water tank	2

Emry K Major
for Officer Commanding
1/21st London Regt.

Appendix I

2/21st BATTALION, THE LONDON REGIMENT

PROGRAMME OF TRAINING FOR THE WEEK COMMENCING 29th May 1916.

MONDAY
29/5/16   7-0 a.m. "A" & "B" Co. Field Firing   9-0 a.m. "C" & "D" Cos. parade for Bayonet Fighting & Physical Training
                                                      2-0 p.m. "C" & "D" Cos. parade for Coy. Training.
                                                      3-30 p.m. "A" & "B" Cos. Bayonet Fighting & Obstacle Course.

TUESDAY
30/5/16   7 -0 a.m. - Drill Parade.   BATTALION UNDER COMMANDING OFFICER.
           7-45 a.m.

WEDNESDAY
31/5/16   ROYAL REVIEW.

THURSDAY
1/6/16   7 -0 - Drill Parade   9-0 a.m. Coys. Parade for Bayonet Fighting,   2-0 p.m. C & D. Cos. Field Firing.
         7-45 a.m.   Bomb Throwing etc.   2-0 p.m. A & B. Cos. parade for Coy. Training.

FRIDAY
2/6/16   7 -0 - Drill Parade   BATTALION TRAINING
        7-45 a.m.

SATURDAY
3/6/16   7 -0 - Drill Parade   9-0 a.m. Interior Economy
         7-45 a.m.

SUNDAY
4/6/16   CHURCH PARADE.

SUTTON VENY
27th May 1916.

CAPT. & ADJUTANT.
2/21st Battalion,
THE LONDON REGIMENT.

Appendix II

2/21st BATTALION, THE LONDON REGIMENT.

PROGRAMME OF TRAINING FOR WEEK COMMENCING 5th June 1916

MONDAY 5/6/16	7-0 - Drill Parade. 7-45 a.m.	9-0 a.m. & 2-0 p.m. Parade under Company Arrangements.
TUESDAY 6/6/16	7-0 - Drill Parade. 7-45 a.m.	9-0 a.m. & 2-0 p.m. Parade under Company arrangements.
WEDNESDAY 7/6/16	7-0 - Drill Parade. 7-45 a.m.	9-0 a.m. & 2-0 p.m. Parade under Company Arrangements.
THURSDAY 8/6/16	7-0 - Drill Parade. 7-45 a.m.	9-0 a.m. & 2-0 p.m. Parade under Company arrangements.
FRIDAY 9/6/16		BATTALION TRAINING.
SATURDAY 10/6/16	7-0 - Drill Parade. 7-45 a.m.	9-0 a.m. Interior Economy.
SUNDAY 11/6/16		CHURCH PARADE.

During the days when parades are under Company arrangements, special attention must be paid to:-

(1) Bayonet Fighting. (5) Rapid Loading. (8) Through Inspection of small
(2) Physical Training. (6) Bomb Throwing.   Kit.
(3) Obstacle Course.   (7) Rapid Adjustment of Gas (9) Fitting of New Equipment.
(4) Fire Discipline.   Helmets & Goggles.

SUTTON VENY.

4th June 1916.

CAPT. & ADJUTANT.
2/21st Battalion.
THE LONDON REGIMENT.

Appendix IV

2/21st Battalion, THE LONDON REGIMENT.

PROGRAMME OF TRAINING FOR WEEK COMMENCING 12 JUNE 1916

MONDAY 12/6/16	7-0 – 7-45 a.m.	Drill Parade	9-0 a.m. "M" Co. Wiring & Digging 2-0 p.m. B,C,& D Cos. Parade under Company Arrangements	R.A.M.C. Draft Field Firing B & D Cos. Obstacle Course
TUESDAY 13/6/16	7-0 – 7-45 a.m.	Drill Parade	9-0 – 10-30 a.m. 100 men of D Co. Digging 10-30 – 1 p.m. 100 " C Co. " 2-0 – 3-30 p.m. 100 " B Co. " 3-30 – 5-0 p.m. 100 " A Co. "	Physical Training and Bayonet Fighting under Co. Arrangts. C Co. Wiring
WEDNESDAY 14/6/16		8-30 a.m. BATTALION ROUTE MARCH.		
THURSDAY 15/6/16	7-0 – 7-45 a.m.	Drill Parade	9-0 a.m. B Co. Wiring & Digging 2-0 p.m. B Co. " A,C,& D Cos. Parade under Company Arrangements	L.R.B. Draft Instruction in Short Rifle and Wiring A & D Cos. Obstacle Course
FRIDAY 16/6/16	7-0 – 7-45 a.m.	Drill Parade	9-0 a.m. D Co. Wiring & Digging 2-0 p.m. D Co. " A,B,& C Cos. Parade under Company Arrangements.	L.R.B. Draft 25 rounds of Musketry Course R.A.M.C. Draft and men from Prov.Battn. Route March.
SATURDAY 17/6/16	7-0 – 7-45 a.m.	Drill Parade	9-0 a.m. Interior Economy	L.R.B. Draft 25 rounds of Musketry Course R.A.M.C. Draft and men from Prov.Battn. Wiring.
SUNDAY 18/6/16		CHURCH PARADE		

With the exception of Wednesday 14-6-16 companies must carry out 1 hour Bayonet Fighting and 2 hours Physical Training daily. Company Bombers will have ½ hours Throwing Practice daily.
Snipers(under Sniping Officer) and Bombers will carry out their Training under Brigade Arrangements. They will be struck off all duties except route marching. Signallers under Signalling Officer.
On days when Wiring and Digging occur together for one company, one half should carry out Digging and the remainder Wiring in the morning, changing over in the afternoon.

Chas Reynolds
Lieut.& A/Adjutant

Appendix IV

BATTALION ORDERS NO 3 FOR 30/6/16 BY LT. COLONEL B. FLETCHER
COMMANDING 2/21st BATTALION, THE LONDON REGIMENT.

LOUEZ.
30/6/16.

Part 1.

1. **DETAIL** Captain of the day .... Capt. Bloy
   Subaltern of the day .... 2/Lt. Exall

   BATTALION ORDERLIES .... (Sgt. Gillard   A.Co.
                                    (Corpl. Lash   C.Co.

2. **ROUTINE** Reveille   6 a.m.   Dinners   1 p.m.
   Sick Parade   9 a.m.
   Breakfast   8 a.m.

3. **PARADES** The Battalion will move to occupy Trenches (times as per attached move Table).
   "A" Company 100 men   "B" Company 100 men.
   "C" Company 160 men   "D" Company 160 men.
   Grenadier Platoon.   M.G. Section.

   All men not sent up will occupy billets in Sugar Refinery Transport remain in present billets.

4. **SALE OF ALCOHOL** The following extract from Third Army Routine Order No. 451 is published for information :-
   "With reference to Third Army Routine Order 311, dated 21st February 1916, it is to be understood that Officers are included in the prohibition regarding the purchase of alcoholic drinks other than beer, cider, and light wines, at hotels, Cafes etc. in the Third Army Area.

5. **RAILWAYS** The following extract from XVll Army Corp Routine Orders, dated 26th June, 1916, is published for information and strict compliance :-
   "Troops are forbidden to walk along the permanent way of French Railways."

6. **BOMBARDMENT** In the event of heavy bombardment there are trenches at the back of the Sugar Refinery for the use of troops.

7. **GAS ALARM** In the event of the horn under the arch being sounded, it denotes that a gas attack is taking place. All troops will immediately put on their gas helmets. Helmets will not be removed without orders from an Officer.

8. **DISCIPLINE** (1) During the daylight, troops will leave the Sugar Refinery of not more than 10. Troops off duty must not be allowed to wander about the village; they will only leave their billets between the hours of 11 a.m. and 1 p.m., and 6 p.m. and 8 p.m. (unless on duty) for the purpose of proceeding to Estaminets. They must be properly dressed and carry their satchels.
   (2) All notices posted about billets must be obeyed.

9. **SALUTING** The Brigadier-General has again drawn attention the fact that men of this Brigade pay no attention to Staff Officers in motor cars. Men should salute any car that ever looks like containing an Officer. The Brigadier feels sure that he will have no further complaint as to this.

10. **AEROPLANES** On the approach of hostile aircraft, the policeman on duty at the gate will blow 3 blasts on a whistle, which will denote that all troops must immediately get under cover. On 1 blast being blown. It will denote that all is clear.

(Sgd) G. MACDONALD
Capt. & Adjutant
2/21st Battalion,
THE LONDON REGIMENT.

No. 7 to T.O.
 " 8 " Q.M.

(2)

INSTRUCTIONS.

(1) The following trenches are used for traffic "UP" to the trenches only :-

Avenue ANZIN
" BETHUNE
" ANNIVERSAIRE.

The following trenches are used for traffic "DOWN" from the trenches only :-

Avenue GENIE
" MADAGASCAR
" LABYRINTHE

(2) Parties going to or from the trenches must keep in the Communication Trenches N.E. of the ANZIN/ST. CATHERINE Road by day.

Individuals (never more than 5 men together) may move in the open W. of the BETHUNE ROAD. E. of the BETHUNE Road nobody is allowed to move outside the trenches by day.

No wagons are allowed E. of ANZIN CHURCH by day.
Nobody will walk along BETHUNE/ARRAS Rd. BY DAY.

(3) No Transport going up to the Dumps with rations and R.E. material at night are allowed to pass ANZIN. Church before 9-30 p.m.
Strict orders must be issued that there is as little noise as possible at the Dumps and that no lights are allowed after leaving ANZIN. This refers to the striking of matches as well as to the use of electric torches.
It is of the greatest importance that this order is strictly enforced.

CAPT. & ADJUTANT.
2/21st Battalion.
THE LONDON REGIMENT.

TABLE OF MOVES OF THE 2/21st BATTALION, THE LONDON REGT.

UNIT	FROM	TO	POSITION	ATTACHED TO	GUIDES MET	TIME	REMARKS
Grenadier Platoon	Louez	Right 1 Subsector.	Front Line	4th Seaforths' who furnish Guides.	ANZIN CHURCH	2-45 p.m.	
No. 1 Platoon	"	"	"	"	"	3-45 p.m.	
" 2 "	"	"	"	"	"	3-55 p.m.	
" 3 "	"	"	"	"	"	4 -5 p.m.	
" 4 "	"	"	"	"	"	4-15 p.m.	
" 5 "	"	"	"	"	"	4-25 p.m.	
" 6 "	"	"	"	"	"	4-35 p.m.	
" 7 "	"	"	"	"	"	4-45 p.m.	
" 8 "	"	"	"	"	"	4-55 p.m.	
" 9 "	"	Bde. Res.	ABRI. CENTRAL.	TO RELIEVE 2 Coys. 9th Royal Scots who will furnish all guides.	"	5-15 p.m.	
" 10 "	"	"	"	"	"	5-25 p.m.	
" 11 "	"	"	"	"	"	5-35 p.m.	
" 12 "	"	"	ABRI MOUTIN	"	"	5-45 p.m.	
" 13 "	"	"	"	"	"	5-55 p.m.	
" 14 "	"	"	"	"	"	6 -5 p.m.	
" 15 "	"	" "	"	"	"	6-15 p.m.	
" 16 "	"	" "	"	"	"	6-25 p.m.	
Lewis M.G. Section.			1 Gun per Co. attached to Nos. 1, 5, 9 & 13 Platoons.				

Headquarters of the Battalion will be at LOUEZ.
Brigade Reserve will be under command of Major MACKINNON, 4th Gordon Highlanders.
Battalion Medical Aid Post at ABRI MOUTIN.

[signature]
CAPT. & ADJUTANT.
2/21st Battalion,
THE LONDON REGIMENT.

VOLUME 7.

Vol 2

W A R D I A R Y

of the

2/21st BATTALION, THE LONDON REGIMENT.

from

1st JULY 1916 to 31st JULY 1916.

WAR DIARY *1/21st London Regt.* Army Form C. 2118.
or
INTELLIGENCE SUMMARY.
(Erase heading not required.) Reference Maps. France. LENS 11. Scale 1/10000

Place	Date	Hour	Summary of Events and Information	Remarks and references to Appendices
LOUEZ	1916 July 1		Battalion less details (287 N.C.Os & men) in trenches occupied by 154th Brigade 51st Division, for instruction. Weather - fine	See Appendix I
	2		Battalion in trenches for instruction as previous day	
	7	8 p.m.	196 N.C.Os & men on various working parties for 154th Brigade. Weather - fine. Stores received on this day:- 40 Periscopes, vigilant No 18 53 Box respiratory 50 Helmets to P.H.Q 230 Helmets to drill 4 Lewis Guns .303 4 Hoses, magazines	

Army Form C. 2118.

WAR DIARY
2/21st London Regt.
INTELLIGENCE SUMMARY.
(Erase heading not required.) Reference Map FRANCE. LENS 11

Place	Date	Hour	Summary of Events and Information	Remarks and references to Appendices
LOUEZ	1916 July 3		120 N.C.O. men (60 A Coy. & 60 B) were sent to join Battalion in trenches	PM
	4		Battalion under instruction in trenches as previous day. Casualties in trenches — 2 men wounded. Weather — fine.	PM
			Battalion under instruction in trenches as previous day. Casualties in trenches — 1 man wounded. Weather — Wet. Stores received this day 184 magazines, Lewis Guns. 303	PM
	5		Battalion under instruction in trenches as previous day. Weather — Showery.	PM

WAR DIARY or INTELLIGENCE SUMMARY

Army Form C. 2118.

2/21st London Regt.

FRANCE. LENS 11.

Place	Date	Hour	Summary of Events and Information	Remarks and references to Appendices
LOVEZ	1916 July 6th		Battalion Headquarters still LOVEZ. Battalion holds instruction in trenches as before. Weather - Showery	
	7		Battalion Headquarters moved to MAROEUIL. Battalion was relieved in trenches by 2/23rd London Regt. and marched to billets in MAROEUIL. Casualties - 1 man wounded. Weather - Showery	
MAROEUIL 8			Battalion marched back again to CHELERS. Weather - Fine	On App II
CHELERS 9 & 10			Cleaning up & in billets. Weather - Fine. Stores received on 10th & Periscopes No 9 & 64 cutters, wire No 1 Fatigue parties, Bombing, Rapid Wiring, Bayonet fighting on. Weather fine	
CHELERS 11			Stores received this day 350 Helmets, steel	

Army Form C. 2118

WAR DIARY 2/21st London Regt.
INTELLIGENCE SUMMARY
(Erase heading not required.) Reference Maps FRANCE, LENS 11.

Place	Date 1916	Hour	Summary of Events and Information	Remarks and references to Appendices
CHELERS	July 12	8 a.m.	Fatigue parties. Rapid wiring, Gas helmet Instruction. Consolidation of Trenches at AGNIERES (Ref 52 Sheet 51 C) 100 all ranks of C Company + 100 all ranks D Company = 200 total. Weather – Fine	
CHELERS	13	9 a.m.	Battalion marched to ETRUN arriving 3.15 p.m. – Route TINQUES – SAVY – HAUTE AVESNES. Weather – Showery Strength 350 Limits (total, revised on 11th inst.; sent over under Brigade arrangements) Battalion in billets	
ETRUN	14		Battalion less 1 Company (A) – Divisional Reserve 1 Company (A) – Brigade Reserve Weather – Fine Stores received this day	
			27 Rifles Grenades	
ETRUN	15		Battalion in billets as in previous day Weather – Fine The following Officers from Reserve Battalion reported 2nd Lt C.B. WARD, T.H. ABRAHALL & F.G. HODGE. Stores received this day 40 Pairs Coffee N° 18 Vigilent 48 Hedging gloves	

Army Form C. 2118

WAR DIARY 2/21st London Regt.
or
INTELLIGENCE SUMMARY Ref. Map. FRANCE. LENS 11
(Erase heading not required.)

Instructions regarding War Diaries and Intelligence Summaries are contained in F. S. Regs., Part II. and the Staff Manual respectively. Title Pages will be prepared in manuscript.

Erale cut 100000

Place	Date	Hour	Summary of Events and Information	Remarks and references to Appendices
ETRUN	1916 July 17		Battalion relieved 2/23rd London Regt. in Right sector Trenches No. 1 Ref. Map ROCLINCOURT. 51.B N.W.1 Weather - showery. Stores received this day 800 Helmets to steel.	Appendix III
			Battalion in trenches. Disposition - A & B Companies in front line - BONNAL L 20 - L 28 C & D in Support. GRAND COLLECTEUR. Some shelling took place otherwise day was quiet. Casualties 2 men killed, 3 wounded Weather - Unsettled.	
	18		Battalion in trenches. Towards end of afternoon, right sector of BONNAL was badly damaged by Still pipe, near L 22 - otherwise day passed quietly. Casualties - 1 killed 5 wounded. Weather - fine.	

WAR DIARY or INTELLIGENCE SUMMARY

Army Form C. 2118

2/21st London Regt.
Ref. Map FRANCE. LENS 11 Scale 1/10000

Place	Date	Hour	Summary of Events and Information	Remarks and references to Appendices
	July 1916 19		Battalion in trenches. Fairly heavy shelling took place early this morning chiefly directed against BOYAU about Sap 23. During the night 18/19 trench mortars left of Sap 22 damaged. Previous day were repaired. Weather - Fine.	RM
	20	12noon	Battalion in trenches. Relief by 2/23rd London Regt. from Reserve commenced. Disposition of Battalion in Reserve. A Company — ABRI CENTRALE under orders of 2/23rd London Regt. 'A' Battalion B " — ECURIE défense. C " — JUNKEN ROAD under orders of 2/24th London Regt. 'B' Battalion D " — ABRI MOUTON. Relief was delayed somewhat owing to shelling by the enemy. Casualties. 1 Killed 5 wounded. Weather - Fine. Hot.	RM

Army Form C. 2118

WAR DIARY
or
INTELLIGENCE SUMMARY
2/21st London Regt.
Inf. Bde. FRANCE LENS II
ROCLINCOURT 57B N.W.1.

(Erase heading not required.)

Instructions regarding War Diaries and Intelligence Summaries are contained in F. S. Regs., Part II. and the Staff Manual respectively. Title Pages will be prepared in manuscript.

Place	Date 1916	Hour	Summary of Events and Information	Remarks and references to Appendices
ECURIE	July 21		Battalion in reserve. 2nd Lt. H.S. ROBINSON reported from Reserve Battalion. Weather - fine.	Pw
	22		Battalion in reserve. Casualty - 1 wounded (accidently). Weather - fine.	Pw
	23	11.30 p.m. until 6 a.m. 24/7/16	Battalion in reserve. Company in ECURIE defences stood to. Weather - fine.	Pw
	24		Battalion in reserve. Weather - fine. dull	Pw
	25		Battalion in reserve. Weather - fine.	Pw
	26		Battalion in reserve. Weather - fine.	Pw

WAR DIARY 2/21st London Regt.
or
INTELLIGENCE SUMMARY Reg. Mgr. FRANCE LENS 11 Scale
(Erase heading not required.) ROCLINCOURT 51B N.W.1   1/100,000

Army Form C. 2118

Place	Date 1916	Hour	Summary of Events and Information	Remarks and references to Appendices
ECURIE	July 27		Battalion in reserve. Weather – fine	Pm
ECURIE	28		Battalion relieved in reserve trenches by 2/24th London Regt. Battalion relieves 2/23rd London Regt in front line and support trenches RIGHT 1 sector. Disposition of Battalion – C & D Companies in front line, BONNAL – A & B Companies in support, GRAND COLLECTEUR. Draft of 20 men from Reserve Battalion reported. Weather – fine	Pm
RIGHT 1 sector				
ETRUN				Pm
RIGHT 1 sector	29	5.30 p.m.	Battalion in trenches. Arrival of draft of 20 men to join battalion in trenches. Weather – fine	Pm
	30		Battalion in trenches. Weather – fine, hot	Pm
	31		Battalion in trenches. Weather – fine, hot.	

P.J. Fletcher, Lieut Col.
Commanding 2/21st London Regt

Appendix I
Copyright Major

TABLE OF MOVES OF 2/21st BATTALION, THE LONDON REGIMENT

UNIT	FROM	TO	POSITION	ATTACHED TO	REMARKS
Grenadier Platoon	Louez	Right 1 Subsector	Front Line	154th Inf. Brigade.	On 3rd July Platoons Nos. 9 to 16 changed places in Front Line with Nos. 1 to 8 Platoons, who then went to Brigade Reserve.
No. 1 Platoon	"	"	"	"	
" 2	"	"	"	"	
" 3	"	"	"	"	
" 4	"	"	"	"	
" 5	"	"	"	"	
" 6	"	"	"	"	
" 7	"	"	"	"	
" 8	"	Bde. Res.	ABRI. CENTRAL	"	
" 9	"	"	"	"	
" 10	"	"	"	"	
" 11	"	"	ABRI MOUTIN.	"	
" 12	"	"	"	"	
" 13	"	"	"	"	
" 14	"	"	"	"	
" 15	"	"	"	"	
" 16	"	"	"	"	
Lewis M.G. Sectn.	"	"	1 Gun per Co. attached to Nos. 1, 5, 9 & 13 Platoons.	"	

Headquarters of the Battalion will be at LOUEZ.
Brigade Reserve will be under command of Major MACKINNON, 4th Gordon Highlanders.
Battalion Medical Aid Post at ABRI MOUTON.

BATTALION ORDERS NO. 4 for 8/7/16 BY LT. COL. B.FLETCHER
COMMANDING 2/21st BATTALION, THE LONDON REGIMENT.
                                                    IN THE FIELD
                                                    7th July 1916.
                PART 1.

1. ROUTINE   Breakfast (under Co. arrangements) before 9 a.m.
              Dinners   ditto   before leaving.

2. PARADES BATHS   Companies will bathe at times as under :-
            "C" Company   1 Platoon to arrive at Baths   9 -0 a.m.
                          1   "   "   "   9-15 a.m.
                          1   "   "   "   9-30 a.m.
                          1   "   "   "   9-45 a.m.
            "B" COMPANY   1   "   "   "   10-15 a.m.
                          1   "   "   "   10-30 a.m.
            "A" Company   1   "   "   "   11 -0 a.m.
                          1   "   "   "   11-15 a.m.
            "D" Company   1   "   "   "   11-45 a.m.
                          1   "   "   "   12 -0 noon
                          1   "   "   "   12-15 p.m.
                          1   "   "   "   12-30 p.m.

    CONSOLIDATION CRATERS PARTY
                                Marching Out
    1 Platoon "B" Company (1 Officer & 50 men)   7-15 a.m.
    1   "   "   "   "   "   7-20 a.m.
    1   "   "A"   "   "   "   7-25 a.m.
    1   "   "   "   "   "   7-30 a.m.
         Intervals of 300 yards to be maintained between
    Platoons.
    ROUTE   BRAY - ACQ - CAPELLE-FERMONT - AGNIERES (E.2 Sheet
    51 C).
         Capt. English and 2 Officers in Command of "B" Company
         Major Puckle and 2 Officers in Command of "A" Company.
       One Field Cooker with rations will accompany this Party
       One cook per Company to accompany Cooker, which will
    follow rear platoon.
         On completion of Instruction this Party will proceed to
    CHELERS to rejoin Battalion.

    BATTALION MOVE   MAROEUIL - CHELERS
         The Battalion will parade as under ready to move off
    at the time stated :-
    ROUTE   BRAY - ACQ - Cross Road N. of HAUTE AVESNES -
            ARRAS - ST. POL Road - SAVY - TINCQUES - CHELERS.
         From MAROEUIL to ACQ the Battalion will move by
    Platoons at 300 yards distance, Transport will move by
    single wagons at same distance as far as ACQ.

    ORDER OF MARCH   Pass Starting
                                                  Point.
    Advance Guard (1 Platoon "B" Co.   1-27 p.m.
                  (1 Platoon "B" Co.   1-30 p.m.
                   Headquarters & Signallers   1-33 p.m.
                   1 Platoon "A" Co.   1-36 p.m.
                   1   ditto   1-39 p.m.
                   1 Platoon "C" Co.   1-42 p.m.
                   1   ditto   1-45 p.m.
                   1   ditto   1-48 p.m.
                   1   ditto   1-51 p.m.
                   1 Platoon "D" Co.   1-54 p.m.
                   1   ditto   1-57 p.m.
                   1   ditto   2 -0 p.m.
                   1   ditto   2- 3 p.m.
                   M.G.Section   2 -6 p.m.
         Transport with intervals of 300 yards between wagons.
         The above formation will be maintained until reaching
    "LE CABARET BLANC" on the ARRAS/ST. POL Road, where Platoons
    will halt until Battalion forms up.

(2)

Watches will be set by Signallers time 12 noon.
All Field Cookers must be ready to move by 2 p.m.
One Field Cooker will be shared by "A" & "B" $\frac{1}{2}$ Companies.
Water Bottles will be filled from Water Carts at times as under :-

        "C" Co. by Platoons   10 - 11 a.m.
        "B" Co.   "   11-30 a.m. - 12 noon
        "A" Co.   "   12 noon - 12-30 p.m.
        "D" Co.   "   8-30 - 9-30 a.m.

Water carts are behind No. 36 ECURIE ROAD.

<u>BILLETING PARTY</u> Capt. Brett and 1 Sergt, per Company will report to the Adjutant at 11 a.m. at Battalion Headquarters. All must be able to ride Bicycles.

CAPT. & ADJUTANT.
2/21st Battalion,
THE LONDON REGIMENT.

Bn. Appendix III

SECRET

OPERATION ORDER NO. 2 BY LT. COLONEL B. FLETCHER

16th July 1916.

The Battalion will move from ETRUN to relieve the 2/23rd Battalion, The Lond. Regt. in Right Sector Trenches No. 1.

DISPOSITIONS   "A" Company - BONNAL Trench   Right
                    "B" Company - BONNAL Trench   Left.
                    "C" Company - COLLECTEUR Trench Right.
                    "D" Company - COLLECTEUR Trench Left.

STARTING POINT Bridge over Stream on ETRUN - LOUEZ Road.

ORDER OF MARCH   Time to pass Starting Point

1 Officer per Coy.)		
R.S.Major)	Advance Party	~~9-0 a.m.~~
4 C.S.Majors)		9 -0 a.m.
M.G. Section		9-15 a.m.
Signal Section		9-30 a.m.
Headquarters		10-30 a.m.
No. 1 Platoon		12-0 noon
No. 2 "		12-2 p.m.
No. 3 "		12-4 p.m.
No. 4 "		12-6 p.m.
No. 5 "		12-8 p.m.
No. 6 "		12-10 p.m.
No. 7 "		12-12 p.m.
No. 8 "		12-14 p.m.
No. 9 "		12-16 p.m.
No. 10 "		12-18 p.m.
No. 11 "		12-20 p.m.
No. 12 "		12-22 p.m.
No. 13 "		12-24 p.m.
No. 14 "		12-26 p.m.
No. 15 "		12-28 p.m.
No. 16 "		12-30 p.m.

Guides from the 2/23rd Battalion, Lond. Regt for each Platoon will be met at ANZIN CHURCH.

Brigade time will be ascertained at Battalion Headquarters at 9 a.m.
The interval between Platoons will be maintained as far as possible.
Snipers will report at Snipers Dug-Out on arrival, to Brigade Sniping Officer.

Macdonald
CAPT. & ADJUTANT
2/21st Battalion,
THE LONDON REGIMENT.

No. 1 Copy to 181st Inf. Bde.
" 2 "   Filed
" 3 "   "A" Co.
" 4 "   "B" Co.
" 5 "   "C" Co.
" 6 "   "D" Co.
" 7 "   M.G. Section
" 8 "   Signal Section
" 9 "   War Diary.

INSTRUCTIONS

(1) The following trenches are used for traffic "UP" to the trenches only :-

   Avenue ANZIN
   " BETHUNE
   " ANNIVERSAIRE

The following trenches are used for traffic "DOWN" from the trenches only. :-

   Avenue GENIE
   " MADAGASCAR
   " LABYRINTHE

(2) Parties going to or from the trenches must keep in the Communication Trenches N.E. of the ANZIN/ST CATHERINE Road by day.

Individuals (never more than 5 men together) may move on the open W. of the BETHUNE ROAD. E. of the BETHUNE Road nobody is allowed to move outside the trenches by day.

No wagons are allowed E. of ANZIN Church by day. Nobody will walk along BETHUNE/ARRAS RD. by day.

(3) No Transport going up to the Dumps with rations and R.E. material at night are allowed to pass ANZIN Church before 9-30 p.m.
Strict orders must be issued that there is as little noise as possible at the Dumps and that no lights are allowed after leaving ANZIN. This refers to the striking of matches as well as to the use of electric torches.
It is of the greatest importance that this order is strictly enforced.

        (Sgd) G.MACDONALD.
          CAPT. & ADJUTANT.
          2/21st Battalion,
          THE LONDON REGIMENT

Volume 8

Vol III

War Diary
of the
2/21st Battalion, London Regiment
from
1st to 31st August 1916.

Confidential

WAR DIARY
or
INTELLIGENCE SUMMARY

1/21st London Regt.
FRANCE. LENS 11
ROCLINCOURT 57B N.W.1 Edition 2. d

Army Form C. 2118

Place	Date	Hour	Summary of Events and Information	Remarks and references to Appendices
	1916 Aug 1		Battalion in trenches. Change in disposition – A Coy relieved C, in Spring Line (BONNAY). C Coy then went into Supports (GRAND COLLECTEUR). B Coy relieved D in Spring Line (BONNAL). D Coy then went into Supports (GRAND COLLECTEUR). Various troops without any European front line, Listening on them, have appeared in the German front line. Weather fine, hot.	Dr.
	2		Battalion in trenches. Rather more than usual Grand mortar activity by the enemy. Two guns of C. Battery 322nd R.G.A. Brigade bombarded the German wire in front of their first line for about 30 minutes from 5 p.m., as an experiment to create gaps in wire for our patrols, giving to sweep after dark. This took place in front of BONNAL. Opposite our line & between SAPS 20 & 21. Casualties 2 killed, 5 wounded (2 W6 Coy & 3 men) Weather – fine, hot.	Dr.
	3		Battalion in trenches. Weather fine.	

Army Form C. 2118

2/12th London Regt.
Rd. Hqrs. FRANCE, LENS 11 sheets
ROCLINCOURT S13.B N.W.1 Edition 2 d 70000

WAR DIARY
or
INTELLIGENCE SUMMARY
(Erase heading not required.)

Instructions regarding War Diaries and Intelligence Summaries are contained in F.S. Regs., Part II. and the Staff Manual respectively. Title Pages will be prepared in manuscript.

Place	Date	Hour	Summary of Events and Information	Remarks and references to Appendices
	1916 Aug			
ETRUN	4		Battalion in trenches. Casualties – 2 men wounded. Arrival draft of 25 men from Reserve Battalion at rear Headquarters. Weather – fine	RM
ETRUN	5		Battalion relieved in trenches by 2/23rd London Regiment. Headquarters moved to rear Headquarters. Weather – fine	RM
ETRUN	6		Battalion in rest billets. Weather – fine	RM
ETRUN	7		Battalion in rest billets. 2nd Lt E.H. TIDDY reported from Reserve Battalion. Weather – fine	RM
"	8		Battalion in rest billets. Weather – fine	RM
"	9		Battalion in rest billets. Casualty – 1 wounded accidental (bomb throwing instruction). Weather – fine	RM

Army Form C. 2118

WAR DIARY 3/1st London Regt.
or
INTELLIGENCE SUMMARY Ruf. Map FRANCE LENS 11
(Erase heading not required.) ROCLINCOURT 51.B. N.W. 1 Edition C

Instructions regarding War Diaries and Intelligence Summaries are contained in F.S. Regs., Part II. and the Staff Manual respectively. Title Pages will be prepared in manuscript.

Place	Date 1916	Hour	Summary of Events and Information	Remarks and references to Appendices
ETRUN	Aug 10		Battalion in rest billets. 2nd Lt. J.P. COYLE reported from Reserve Battalion. Weather - fine	RW
	11		Battalion in rest billets. Casualties - 1 killed + 1 wounded (both whilst undergoing bomb throwing instruction) Weather - fine	RW
	12		Battalion in rest billets. Capt. H.C. LEMAN reported from 3/25th London Regt. Weather - fine	RW
	13		Battalion relieved 2/23rd London Regt. in trenches. Dispositions in trenches C Coy. in firing line (BONNAL) D " " " " " " A " " " Support (COLLECTEUR) B " " " " Satisfactory relief carried out. Weather - fine	RW

Army Form C. 2118

WAR DIARY
or
INTELLIGENCE SUMMARY
(Erase heading not required.)

21st London Regt
FRANCE. LENS 11
Ref. Maps ROCLINCOURT 51.B N.W.I. Edition 2.d 1/10000

Place	Date	Hour	Summary of Events and Information	Remarks and references to Appendices
	Aug 1916 14		Battalion in Trenches. Considerable Trench Mortar activity on part of enemy, front line (BONNAL trench) rather knocked about. Parties forming made during night 14/15th August with re-wiring etc. front of front trench. Casualties – 1 man wounded. Weather – Showery.	P.M.
	15		Battalion in Trenches. Day passed quietly. Usual amount of shelling by enemy Trench Mortars. Weather – Showery. Heavy rain during afternoon.	P.M.
	16	9.30 p.m	Battalion in Trenches. Bombardment by Brigade Artillery on enemy's lines in front of SAPS 21, L 23. Enemy immediately replied, by this bombardment nothing of importance took place. 2nd Lieuts. S.A. MORGAN JONES and C.F.B. MARTIN reported from Reserve (3/21st) Battalion. Casualties – 2 men killed 3 wounded. ETRUN – 1 man injured (accidental). At our headquarters Weather – Showery.	P.M.

WAR DIARY
or
INTELLIGENCE SUMMARY

Army Form C. 2118

1/21st London Regt.
FRANCE. LENS 11 South 1/100,000
ROCLINCOURT SIB NW1 Edition 2.C.

Place	Date 1916	Hour	Summary of Events and Information	Remarks and references to Appendices
	Aug 17		Battalion in trenches. Change in disposition A Coy relieved G support line (BONNAL) then went into support (GRAND COLLECTEUR) C: then went D support line (BONNAL) B: relieved D in front line (BONNAL) D: went into support (GRAND COLLECTEUR) Nothing of importance took place. Weather - Showery.	RM
	18		Relief carried out quietly. Casualties - 1 O.R wounded. Weather - Showery.	
	19		Battalion in trenches. Enemy reported to have trench mortars being inclined during the night, considerable activity of own artillery took place. Enemy fire arms - 4.30 a.m on 20/8/16 Casualties - 3 O.R. wounded Weather - Showery.	RM
ETRUN	20		Battalion in trenches Arrival of draft of 4 men from Reserve Battalion, at Rear headquarters. Weather - Fine.	RM

Army Form C. 2118

WAR DIARY
or
INTELLIGENCE SUMMARY

2/21st London Regiment
Reg. No. FRANCE LENS 11 Sept
Roclincourt 51.B N.W.1 Edition 2d 1/10000

(Erase heading not required.)

Instructions regarding War Diaries and Intelligence Summaries are contained in F.S. Regs., Part II. and the Staff Manual respectively. Title Pages will be prepared in manuscript.

Place	Date 1916	Hour	Summary of Events and Information	Remarks and references to Appendices
	Aug 21		Battalion leaves the front support line trenches, being relieved by the 2/23rd London Regiment. Relief carried out quietly. Headquarters moved to Brigade Reserve area called "C" Battalion. Disposition of Battalion in Reserve: A Company — ABRI CENTRAL B Company — Headquarters — ECURIE defences C " — SUNKEN ROAD D " — ABRI MOUTON. Arrival of draft of 4 men to join Battalion in the trenches. Weather — Fine	
	22		Battalion in reserve trenches Weather — Fine	Pm
	23		Battalion in reserve trenches Casualty — 1 man wounded Weather — Fine	Pm
	24		Battalion in reserve trenches Weather — Fine	Pm
	25		Battalion in reserve trenches Weather — Fine	Pm

Army Form C. 2118

WAR DIARY
or
INTELLIGENCE SUMMARY

Regiment: 2/21st London Regiment
Reg. Maps FRANCE LENS. 11
ROCLINCOURT 51.B N.W.1 Edition 2.C. Scale 1/100,000

(Erase heading not required.)

Instructions regarding War Diaries and Intelligence Summaries are contained in F.S. Regs., Part II. and the Staff Manual respectively. Title Pages will be prepared in manuscript.

Place	Date 1916	Hour	Summary of Events and Information	Remarks and references to Appendices
	Aug 26		Battalion in reserve trenches. Weather - showery. 2nd Lieut. A.L. HOCKEY reported from Reserve Battalion	An
	27		Battalion in reserve trenches. Weather - showery.	An
	28		Battalion returns in reserve trenches. Weather - showery	An
	29		Battalion relieves 2/23rd London Regt in front support line of RIGHT sector. Disposition C company in firing line (BONNEL) D " " " " A " " support " (GRAND COLLECTEUR) B " " " " Casualties - 2. O.R. wounded Weather - stormy	An
	30		Battalion in trenches. Weather - stormy	An

Army Form C. 2118

WAR DIARY
or
INTELLIGENCE SUMMARY

2/2nd London Regt.
Reg. Map. FRANCE LENS, 11
(Erase heading not required.) ROUNDCOURT S1.B N.W.1 Edition 2.C

Instructions regarding War Diaries and Intelligence Summaries are contained in F.S. Regs., Part II. and the Staff Manual respectively. Title Pages will be prepared in manuscript.

Place	Date 1916	Hour	Summary of Events and Information	Remarks and references to Appendices
	Aug 31		Battalion in trenches. Weather – fine.	By
			B. Fletcher. Lt. Col. Commanding 2/2 st London Regt.	

Volume IX

Vol 4

War Diary
of the
2/21st Battalion, London Regiment
from
1st to 30th September 1916.

Confidential

WAR DIARY or INTELLIGENCE SUMMARY

Army Form C. 2118

(Erase heading not required.)

"Secret" Trench {Army Form ROUINTOUET
Reference { French Map 51B: NW.1. Edition 2c. 1/10,000.

Instructions regarding War Diaries and Intelligence Summaries are contained in F.S. Regs., Part II. and the Staff Manual respectively. Title Pages will be prepared in manuscript.

Place	Date	Hour	Summary of Events and Information	Remarks and references to Appendices
In front line trenches	1st September 1916	—	Major H.C. LEMAN assumed appointment as Second in Command of the Battalion and Major S. Wright had to command "C" Company.	
			Battalion in front line trenches SECT R1. Situation normal. R.E. engaged in fitting Gas Cylinders — front line trench. BONNAL.	
	2nd		Enemy carried out an attempted bombardment of Bn trenches and near headquarters at ETRUN. Bombs who done to BONNAL front line trench and 6 communication trenches and one casualty occurred at ETRUN.	
	3rd		Situation normal. Artillery & Trench Mortars active — wire cutting. 2nd Lieut H.C. COWPER reported for duty on his return from England.	
	4th.	a.m	2/22nd Battalion LONDON Regt. on our left continued a raid on enemy's front line trenches which was repelled on our trenches and the occupation of Trench Mortars and Artillery Gold was unsuccessful owing to the left having been difficult cut.	
		p.m	Bn Battalion was relieved by 1/22nd Battalion LONDON Regt and returned to rest billets at ETRUN. No casualties occurred during relief.	
ETRUN	5th		In rest billets. Captain A.J. WALTER reported from 2nd Army School of Instruction.	
	6th		In rest billets.	
		p.m	Carrying party relieved all night in carrying dry rations from PILLE and ARIANE dumps to divisional list J.R. OXENDEN left for England to join Machine Gun Corps. 2 Lieut J.P. CARR ill for duty with 2nd Survey Coy. R.E. BROUGHAM	

1875 Wt.W593/826 1,000,000 4/15 J.B.C. & A. A.D.S.S./Forms/C. 2118.

Army Form C. 2118

WAR DIARY
or
INTELLIGENCE SUMMARY
(Erase heading not required.)

Instructions regarding War Diaries and Intelligence Summaries are contained in F.S. Regs., Part II. and the Staff Manual respectively. Title Pages will be prepared in manuscript.

Place	Date	Hour	Summary of Events and Information	Remarks and references to Appendices
ETRUN	SEPT 7th	p.m.	In rear billets. Carrying party engaged all night in our 6th.	
	8th		In rear billets.	
		p.m	Carrying party engaged all night as on 6th & 7th.	
	9th		In rear billets	
In front line trenches	10th	12 noon	Battalion relieved 2/23rd Battn. London Regiment in "A" position. No casualties occurred during relief. 2/Lieut. ROBINSON wounded at 12 noon while acting with T.M. Battery.	
		11.30 pm	Patrol under 2/Lieut. SAVORIN encountered hostile patrol in NO MANS LAND but succeeded in driving them off.	
	11th	3 a.m.	Artillery activity on our left. 2/Lieuts 29th and ROB Pongdera carrying out raids on enemy trenches. At same time enemy patrol tried entry SAP 20 but were unsuccessful. Enemy artillery retaliation did some damage to BONNAL and caused 3 casualties :- L/Serjt LASH killed and 2 men wounded.	
		2 p.m.	Enemy shelled BONNAL doing some damage, and killing 2 men. between 6.20 & 6.21. Capt. CLEGG, RAMC, reported to relieve Capt COLE sick.	
		6 p.m.	Installation of Gas cylinders which was to have commenced tonight indefinitely postponed but Orders received that shell of German wire is to be cut and kept open.	

WAR DIARY
or
INTELLIGENCE SUMMARY

(Erase heading not required.)

Army Form C. 2118

Instructions regarding War Diaries and Intelligence Summaries are contained in F. S. Regs., Part II. and the Staff Manual respectively. Title Pages will be prepared in manuscript.

Place	Date	Hour	Summary of Events and Information	Remarks and references to Appendices
In front line trenches	SEPT. 11th	11 pm	A continued style of enemy front line, support line and communication carried out by T.M.s, Stokes, Machine Guns and 18 pdrs. on whole Battalion front. Very little retaliation by the enemy.	
-"-	12th		Enemy heavily bombarded BONNAL during the afternoon causing some material damage but no casualties. Otherwise situation normal. 2/Lieut. A. TEAROE reported for duty; posted to D Company.	
-"-	13th		A quiet morning but about noon enemy bombarded with T.M.s the BONNAL strand causing some damage to the trench and 150 casualties - 1 killed and 1 wounded. 18 pdrs. and 2" T.M. continued wire cutting, throughout the day.	
-"-	14th		Intercompany relief took place during the afternoon. 2 Lieut. H.A. DoCoppet arrived in afternoon. Our T.M.s and artillery carried on a continued style of enemy wire and support trenches. There was practically no retaliation.	
-"-	15th		Wire cutting continued. Enemy retaliated with T.M. damaging BONNAL trench at L22 and L24.	

WAR DIARY
or
INTELLIGENCE SUMMARY

(Erase heading not required.)

Army Form C. 2118

Instructions regarding War Diaries and Intelligence Summaries are contained in F. S. Regs., Part II. and the Staff Manual respectively. Title Pages will be prepared in manuscript.

Place	Date	Hour	Summary of Events and Information	Remarks and references to Appendices
In front line trenches	Sept. 16th	5 pm	Wire cutting continued. Battalion was into Brigade Reserve being relieved by 2/23rd Bn London Regt. No casualties occurred during the relief.	
ECURIE	17th to 22nd		Battalion in Bde Reserve. 2/Lt SOUTHIN and 2/Lt TOWNEND reconnoitred No Man's Land in view of approaching raid on enemy trenches.	
	22nd	pm	Battalion relieved 2/23rd Bn London Regt in front line trenches. No casualties occurred during relief.	
In front line trenches	23rd	am	A quiet morning, but cutting continued by T.M. and artillery.	
		10.20 pm	The Battalion attempted a raid on the enemy front line trenches, the party being under command of 2/Lt SOUTHIN assisted by 2/Lt TOWNEND and 2/Lt HAMILTON. The raid was unsuccessful owing to strong opposition being encountered and 2/Lt TOWNEND had Sgt LINE were killed on the enemy parapet. Search parties under 2/Lt SOUTHIN and 2/Lt TIDDY succeeded in bringing in 2/Lt TOWNEND and 2/Lt LINE's body but Sgt LINE's body had to be left. 2/Lt TIDDY was wounded and 2/Lt TOWNEND died at the 42nd C.C.S. Great gallantry during these assault operations was shown by Sgt WESLEY. Other casualties	

Army Form C. 2118

WAR DIARY
or
INTELLIGENCE SUMMARY
(Erase heading not required.)

Instructions regarding War Diaries and Intelligence Summaries are contained in F. S. Regs., Part II. and the Staff Manual respectively. Title Pages will be prepared in manuscript.

Place	Date	Hour	Summary of Events and Information	Remarks and references to Appendices
In front line trenches	SEPT. 24th		A quiet day with usual T.M. and artillery activity on both sides. During the evening enemy M.G.s fired on LILLE ROAD dump for about two hours.	
	25th to 26th		Battalion in front line trenches: situation abnormally quiet and enemy sent back very little retaliation to our continuous T.M. and artillery fire. An entire company relief took place on 25th Sept. without any casualties.	
	27th		1st S.A.F. Nearly missed no casualties.	
	28th pm		Battalion relieved by 1/23rd Battalion London Regt. and went into Divisional reserve at ETRUN. No casualties during relief.	
ETRUN	29th 30th		Battalion in rest at ETRUN.	

H.B[?]
Major
N.O.C. 2/2nd Bn. London Regt.

30/9/1916

VOLUME X

Vol 5

W A R   D I A R Y

of the

2/21st BATTALION, LONDON REGIMENT

From 1/10/16 to 31/10/16

CONFIDENTIAL

WAR DIARY or INTELLIGENCE SUMMARY

Army Form C. 2118

2/3rd (Postal) London Regiment (First Seven (Rifles))

Reference: Trench Maps. LENS No. 11. 1/10,000

Place	Date	Hour	Summary of Events and Information	Remarks and references to Appendices
ETRUN	October 1st to 3rd		Clocks from "Summer" to Greenwich Time. Battalion in Divisional rooms. On the morning of the 1st October the Battalion was to have been inspected by the Corps Commander Major Gen. S. C. Ferguson, but owing to the very wet weather the parade was cancelled.	Move Order No. 12.
	4th		Battalion relieved 2/2nd Bn London Regt in front line trenches. Weather very wet and trenches – both BONAR and COURCELETTE in badly damaged condition owing to rain. Enemy not about, but a few but little.	
	5th	9.30pm	A raiding party fell on SAP 24 and failed too and wounded two men of "B" Company. A quiet day. Our Stokes and T.M. Lads busy but artillery at headbanding their ammunition. In retaliation for his enemy machine gun fire on the LENS road dumps our Medium guns carried out a systematic strafe of enemy dumps during the evening.	
	6th		The Brigade Commander and G.S.O.1 visited the line and discussed with the Commanding Officer Second in Command and Captain Broy preliminary details of a raid to be carried out by A Company during our next tour.	
		8.10pm	Message received that the 35th Division on our right was carrying out a gas attack. Neighbouring troops were taken by the Battalion, but at last moment attack was postponed. A further warning and postponement were received during the night but apparently the wind was too strong, and	

JHL

WAR DIARY
or
INTELLIGENCE SUMMARY
(Erase heading not required.)

Army Form C. 2118

Instructions regarding War Diaries and Intelligence Summaries are contained in F.S. Regs., Part II. and the Staff Manual respectively. Title Pages will be prepared in manuscript.

Place	Date	Hour	Summary of Events and Information	Remarks and references to Appendices
In front line trenches	Oct 7th		Another quiet day. During the afternoon an inter-company relief successfully took place without casualties. Positions of Companies: Front line: right A.C. left B.C. / Support line: right C.C. left D.C.	
		6:30pm	At 6.50 pm message received that the 30th Division were to be off their gas at 8.15 pm but this was subsequently cancelled	
	8th	am	Enemy sent over large numbers of TMs then moved to no damage caused. No 4626 Pte PITT W. A Company went over in full daylight and entered the German front line. He did not return. Whether he was acted under a fit of mental aberration or from bravado is unknown.	
		6:5pm	At 6.5pm the 22nd Bn. London Regt on our immediate left raided the enemy trenches successfully capturing four prisoners. Considerable artillery retaliation was received and on sector counter damaged.	
		8.45pm	At 8.45 pm the 35th Division on our right let off their gas accompanied by artillery support. The enemy in retaliation did considerable damage to the Battalion on our front and to communications trenches	
	9th		A quiet day. Wind about 10 ms per hour. Steady wind.	
	10th		A quiet day. Though the enemy badly damaged our front line with heavy TMs during the afternoon. Battalion having been relieved by the 2/23rd Bn London Regiment went into Brigade Reserve at EECURIE. Companies as follows A ABRI PAXTON, B ECURIE, C SUNKEN ROAD, D ABRI CENTRALE	

Army Form C. 2118

WAR DIARY
or
INTELLIGENCE SUMMARY
(Erase heading not required.)

Instructions regarding War Diaries and Intelligence Summaries are contained in F.S. Regs., Part II. and the Staff Manual respectively. Title Pages will be prepared in manuscript.

Place	Date	Hour	Summary of Events and Information	Remarks and references to Appendices
EOURIE	October 10/16		Battalion in Brigade Reserve. Defences of Eeurie were manned on the 10th. Nothing of importance occurred during the tour. On the night of 14/15 the ADP1 CENTRALE Company relieved us to support Battery. On the 15/10/16 Lt.Col. B.H.N PARSONS vacated the command of the Battalion being followed by Br. Gen. E. E. DeCOSTA. The Field Artillery and the Corps Heavies carried out a continued straff of the enemy T.M. emplacements &c on the morning & afternoon of the 15th.	
	16	pm	The Battalion went back to R1 Subsector relieving the 1/23rd Bn. LONDON Regt. Companies disposed as follows: LEFT FRONT — D Coy. RIGHT FRONT — C Coy. Support — D Coy. Support — A Coy. The Brigadier made a tour of the subsector with the 2nd in Command during the morning	
	17		A quiet day.	
	18		Nothing of importance occurred	
	19	pm	Inter-company relief. Companies disposed as follows: LEFT FRONT — B RIGHT FRONT — A. Support — D Support — C	
	20		Lt.Col. FLETCHER went on 7 days leave. Major W.C. LEMAN assuming command in his absence. Enemy much more active sending over many S.9s and T.Ms. that WARD C.B. A Coy wounded in the head by a sniper while placing an enemy sniping post. Brigadier visited Subsector in the afternoon and interviewed 4 Subject considered for commission.	
		pm	A message received from Brigade that the Division on our left had ordered Bn. Alert, but leaving it to O.C. Battalion to take any action considered necessary. No attack took place during the night.	

gWb/

WAR DIARY or INTELLIGENCE SUMMARY

Army Form C. 2118

Place	Date	Hour	Summary of Events and Information	Remarks and references to Appendices
	21	12.6 pm	Enemy continued sending over S.9.s and T.M.s throughout the day. Order for Gas Alert received from Brigade; all concerned in the subsection notified. Wind, light N.E.	
		3.15 pm	Further message received from Brigade ordering special precautions as Gas known to be installed on Div front. Immediately, especially, informed as per same order, and all concerned again ordered to take special precautions. Stokes guns ammunition taken to alternative emplacements in CONNOSSEUR in case of emergency.	
		4.30 pm	Order received from Brigade cancelling Gas Alert. All concerned warned to resumption of C.O.	
		5 pm	Ground Gas Alert cancelled 5 pm.	
	22	am	O.C. 2nd Canadian M.M. Coy accompanied by 1 officer per Company arrived to see the line and observe various positions preparatory to taking over. G.O.C. 3rd Canadian Division was round subsection with Major LEMAN.	
		pm	An aerial fight took place over our subsection. Enemy aeroplane Scout immolation.	
	23	am	Corps Commander (xvii Corps) visited Battalion HQs in the line. Brigade Commander was round subsection with Major LEMAN.	
			Relief orders published - copies to all concerned.	Relief orders No. 14
		7.30 pm	Company relief took place in the afternoon disposition as follows: left front D, right front C, support B, support A.	
			Relief completed 4 pm without casualties.	

Army Form C. 2118

WAR DIARY
or
INTELLIGENCE SUMMARY
(Erase heading not required.)

Instructions regarding War Diaries and Intelligence Summaries are contained in F. S. Regs., Part II. and the Staff Manual respectively. Title Pages will be prepared in manuscript.

Place	Date	Hour	Summary of Events and Information	Remarks and references to Appendices
	24		A quiet day. Representatives of the 2nd CANADIAN MNTD. RIFLES arrived to take over the demails.	
	25		Battalion relieved by the 2nd CANADIAN MNTD. RIFLES, proceeding after relief to MAROEUIL. No casualties occurred during the relief.	
MAROEUIL	26		Battalion marched to IZEL-LES-HAMEAU	Orders No. 15.
IZEL-LES-HAMEAU	27		Battalion marched to ESTREE-WAMIN and WAMIN	Orders No. 16.
WAMIN		½	Lieut. Colonel and Hon Colonel F.D WATNEY, the Queens Regiment, joined the Battalion and assumed command	
-do-	28		Battalion marched with 81st Inf. Bde. billeting for the night at NEUVILETTE	Order No. 17
NEUVILETTE	29		Battalion marched to AUTHEUX	Order No. 18
AUTHEUX	30		Battalion in rest. C.O. attended a Conference at Brigade Headquarters.	
-do-	31		Battalion in rest. Training programme for the period of rest, including attack practices &c carried on. Farewell Orders from G.O.C. XVII Corps to 60th (Lond) Division published in Battalion Orders. Weather bad, heavy rain, storms and wind.	Orders No. 20

Major
or Cmdg. 2/2nd Bn LONDON Regt.
31/10/1916.

2/21st BATTALION, THE LONDON REGIMENT

BATTALION MOVE ORDERS NO. 12 for 4/10/16.

Reference - Trench Map 51 B N.W.1. Edition 2C.

The Battalion will move from ETRUN to relieve the 2/23rd Battalion London Regiment in Right 1 Sector Trenches tomorrow, 4th inst.

DISPOSITIONS
"C" Company - BONNAL TRENCH Right
"D" Company - BONNAL TRENCH Left
"A" Company - COLLECTEUR Trench Right
"B" Company - COLLECTEUR Trench Left

STARTING POINT Bridge over stream on ETRUN - LOUEZ Road½

ORDER OF MARCH	Pass Starting Point	Route
1 Officer &) 1 Sgt. per Co.)	9 a.m.	
No. 9 Platoon	12-10 p.m.)	ANZIN AVENUE -
" 10 "	12-15 p.m.)	FILATIERS -
" 11 "	12-20 p.m.)	LOWER BIDOT -
" 12 "	12-25 p.m.)	BLANCHARD ↓ CHEMIN CREUX - RIGHT COLLECTEUR AVENUE G.
" 13 "	12-30 p.m.)	AVENUE ANZIN ↓
" 14 "	12-35 p.m.)	FILATIERS - LOWER
" 15 "	12-40 p.m.)	BIDOT - Direct to
" 16 "	12-45 p.m.)	Left front.
" 1 "	12-50 p.m.)	AVENUE ANZIN -
" 2 "	12-55 p.m.)	FILATIERS - LOWER
" 3 "	1-0 p.m.)	BIDOT - BLANCHARD
" 4 "	1-5 p.m.)	CHEMIN CREUX - to Right Support.
" 5 "	1-10 p.m.)	AVENUE ANZIN-
" 6 "	1-15 p.m.)	FILATIERS - LOWER
" 7 "	1-20 p.m.)	BIDOT - BIDOT -
" 8 "	1-25 p.m.)	to Left Support.

Specialist Sections will relieve the corresponding Sections of the 2/23rd Batt. as under :-

Signallers 9-30 a.m.) AVENUE ANZIN -
Snipers & Bombers 10-0 a.m.) FILATIERS - LOWER
BIDOT - BLANCHARD
No Guides will be provided. SABLIER.

Brigade time will be ascertained at Battalion H.Qrs. at 9 a.m.
The intervals between Platoons will be maintained as far as possible.
O.C. Companies will notify Battalion H.Qrs. when relief is complete - together with any casualties.

J. Keeder
Lt. & A/Adjt.
2/21st Lond. Regt.

Copy No. 1 O.C. 2/2rd L.R.
"   " 2 Filed
"   " 3 A.Co.
"   " 4 B.Co.
"   " 5 C.Co.
"   " 6 D.Co.
"   " 7 Signal Section
"   " 8 Snipers
"   " 9 Bombers
"   " 10 War

SECRET.

2/21st. Battalion. THE LONDON REGIMENT.

BATTALION MOVE ORDERS. No. 14. for 25/10/16.

No. 3 War Diary

Headquarters.
23/10/16.

The Battalion will be relieved on the morning of the 25th inst. by the 2nd CANADIAN MOUNTED RIFLES.

Guides will be at ANZIN CHURCH by 9-10 a.m. under 2/Lt. SOUTHIN.
    One Guide per platoon.
    8 Lewis Gun guides - one per team.
    One from Bombers.
    One from Signallers.
    One from Snipers.
These Guides must adhere to the ROUTES as under :-

The order of RELIEF by incoming BATTALION will be SIGNALLERS, BOMBERS, SNIPERS, A Coy. D Coy. C Coy. B Coy.

A Coy. 2nd C.M.R. will relieve "C" Coy. 2/21st. Battalion. L.R. in RIGHT BONNAL, by ANZIN AVENUE - BARRICADE - ROCLINCOURT AVENUE - BIDOT to LEFT BONNAL.

D Coy. 2nd C.M.R. will relieve D Coy. 2/21st. L.R. in LEFT BONNAL by ANZIN AVENUE - BARRICADE - ROCLINCOURT AVENUE - BIDOT - BLANCHARD - CHEMIN CREUX - LEFT COLLECTEUR - AVENUE G to RIGHT BONNAL.

C Coy. 2nd C.M.R. will relieve B Coy. 2/21st. L.R. by ANZIN AVENUE - BARRICADE - ROCLINCOURT AVENUE - BIDOT to LEFT COLLECTEUR.

B Coy. 2nd C.M.R. will relieve A Coy. 2/21st. L.R. in RIGHT COLLECTEUR by ANZIN AVENUE - BARRICADE - ROCLINCOURT AVENUE - BIDOT - BLANCHARD - CHEMIN CREUX to RIGHT COLLECTEUR.

Lewis Gun Section will be relieved by Lewis Gun Teams of 2nd C.M.R. who will march in 2 teams per Company.

SIGNALLERS, BOMBERS & SNIPERS. will be relieved by sections of the 2nd C.M.R. who will march in by ANZIN AVENUE - BARRICADE - ROCLINCOURT AVENUE - BIDOT - BLANCHARD - CHEMIN CREUX.

The greatest care must be taken by all ranks that during this relief every assistance is given to the Canadian Rifles to enable them to understand thoroughly the system we have found most suitable for Stores, Water, Rations, Cooking, Accommodation etc.

No platoon or section is to leave its position in the line until properly relieved.

Certificates signed by an Officer must be obtained that Stores, Dug-outs, Latrines etc. have been handed over in good order.
These will be handed to the Adjutant at MAROEUIL by 6 p.m.

On completion of relief the Battalion will march to Billets at MAROEUIL, leaving the trenches by following routes :-

    SIGNALLERS, BOMBERS & SNIPERS. BLANCHARD - BARRICADE
                                                 GENIE to ANZIN.

    A Coy.   CHEMIN CREUX - BLANCHARD - BARRICADE - GENIE to ANZIN.

    B Coy.   BIDOT - BLANCHARD - BARRICADE - GENIE to ANZIN.

    C Coy.   BOYAU A - BLANCHARD - BARRICADE - GENIE to ANZIN.

    D Coy.   BIDOT - BLANCHARD - BARRICADE - GENIE to ANZIN.

(2).

From ANZIN to MAROEUIL, platoons will move at 5 minute intervals.

Lieut. NELDER will be responsible that the C.Q.M.Sgts. and sufficient Guides are in readiness to conduct platoons & Specialist sections to billets on arrival at MAROEUIL.

The following details will remain with the Canadian Rifles, in the trenches until the morning of the 27th inst.
   2/Lt. Southin.
   1 Sergeant per Company.
   1 N.C.O. each from SIGNALLERS, BOMBERS, SNIPERS, & HEADQUARTER STORES.

A Certificate will be rendered by each platoon Commander to his O.C. Coy. that before entering billets all rifles were unloaded and inspected. O.C. Companies & Specialist Officers will be responsible that Certificates are handed to the Adjutant to this effect by 6 p.m.

Issued at 4.30 pm. 23/10/16.

Macdonald
CAPT. & ADJT.
2/21st. Battalion.
THE LONDON REGIMENT.

Copy No.1 181st. Inf. Bgde.
   " No.2 File
   " No.3 War Diary.
   " No.4 2nd. C.M.R.
   " No.5 2nd. C.M.R.
   " No.6 A Coy. 2/21st. Battn.
   " No.7 B Coy.   Do.
   " No.8 C Coy.   Do.
   " No.9 D Coy.   Do.
   " No.10 Bombers.
   " No.11 Signallers.
   " No.12 Lewis Guns.
   " No.13 Snipers.

BATTALION ORDERS NO. 15 FOR 26/10/16.

HEADQUARTERS,
25/10/16.

1. ROUTINE   Orderly Officer   2/Lt. Aldis
             Orderly Sergeant   Sergt. Fuller

   Reveille   6-30 a.m.   Dinners   12-15 p.m. en route
   Breakfast   7-30 a.m.   Teas   5 -0 p.m.
                              Orderly Room 6-0 p.m.

2. PARADE   Reference Map   LENS 11 1/100,000

   The Battalion will march to-morrow to IZEL LES-HAMEAU.
   Route :- ARRAS-ST.POL ROAD, HERMAVILLE, IZEL LES -HAMEAU.
   Dress :-   Full Marching Order.
   Rations :- Dinners will be cokked on Field Cookers en route
   to be ready at 12 noon. Unexpended portion of the day's
   rations to be carried on the man.
   Order of March :-
       ADVANCED GUARD (2 platoons D.Co. under Lt. BALFOUR)
       Signal Section
       2 Platoons "D" Company
       "C" Company
       "B" Company
       "A" Company (less 1 Platoon)
       Lewis Gun Section
       Transport
       REAR GUARD (1 Platoon "A" Co.) & Regimental Police.

   STARTING POINT :- Level Crossing S.W. of MAROEUIL

   Advanced Guard passes Starting Point at 9-15 a.m.
   Signal Section   do.   9-17 a.m.
   No. 15 Platoon to pass   do   9-19 a.m.
    " 16   "   do   do   9-21 a.m.
    "   9   "   do   do   9-23 a.m.
    " 10   "   do   do   9-25 a.m.
    " 11   "   do   do   9-27 a.m.
    " 12   "   do   do   9-29 a.m.
    " 13   "
    "   5   "   do   do   9-31 a.m.
    "   6   "   do   do   9-33 a.m.
    "   7   "   do   do   9-35 a.m.
    "   8   "   do   do   9-37 a.m.
    "   2   "   do   do   9-39 a.m.
    "   3   "   do   do   9-41 a.m.
    "   4   "   do   do   9-43 a.m.
   Lewis Gun Section   do   9-45 a.m.
   Transport   do   do   10 -0 a.m.
   Rear Guard   do   do   10-30 a.m.

   Each Unit will halt at 10 minutes to the hour and resume
   the march at the hour.

   Brigade time will be circulated to all Officers by
   the Signal Officer by 8 a.m. on 26th inst.

   The intervals of 200 yards will be maintained until
   reaching the point where the HERMAVILLE ROAD is crossed by
   HAUTE AVESNES - AGNEZ LES DUISANS ROAD, WHERE THE BATTALION
   will form up in column of route and move as a Unit with
   advanced and rear guards.

   Whistle Signals will be used as laid down in
   Divisional Orders.

DISCIPLINE The strictest march discipline must be maintained throughout the march vide Divisional and Brigade memoranda circulated to all Companies.

The contents of above memoranda are to be communicated to all ranks on parade before moving off, and any man not complying with this order must be severely dealt with.

BILLETS The greatest care is to be taken that Billets and ground in the neighbourhood of Billets, Latrines and Cooking Places are clean and tidy.

Macdonald
CAPT. & ADJUTANT.
2/21st BATTALION,
THE LONDON REGIMENT.

BATTALION ORDERS No. 16 for 27/10/16.

Headquarters,
26/10/16.

1. ROUTINE Orderly Officer   2/Lt. Antrobus
            Orderly Sergt.   Sergt. White

            Reveille   6-30 a.m.   Dinners   on arrival
            Sick Parade   6-45 a.m.   Teas   5 p.m.
            Breakfast   7-30 a.m.   Orderly Room 6 p.m.

2. PARADES Reference :- Map LENS 11 1/100,000.

    The Battalion will parade at 9-30 a.m. in CHURCH St. and march to-morrw to ETREE WAMIN.

    ROUTE :- GIVENCHY-le-NOBLE - LIGNEREUIL - to cross roads at T in LIENCOURT - LIENCOURT - ETREE WAMIN.

    The unexpended portion of the day's rations will be carried on the man.

    ORDER OF MARCH :-
            Advanced Guard (2 platoons A.Co. under Capt.
                                                    (Bloy
            Signal Section
            2 Platoons A.Co.
            B.Company
            C.Company
            D.Company (less 1 Platoon)
            Lewis Gun Section.
            Transport
            Rear Guard (1 Platoon D.Co) and Regimental
                                                Police.

    DISCIPLINE   The stricted march discipline must be maintained throughout the march vide Divisional and Brigade Memoranda circulated to all Companies.

    The contents of above memoranda are to be communicated to all ranks on parade before moving off and any man not complying with this order must be severely dealt with.

    BILLETS   The greatest care is to be taken that Billets and ground in the neighbourhood of billets, latrines, and cooking places are left clean and tidy.

                                        Macdonald
                                        CAPT. & ADJUTANT
                                        2/21st Lond. Regt.

WAR DIARY

BATTALION ORDERS NO. 17 for 28/10/16 BY COLONEL F.D.WATNEY
COMMANDING 2/21st BATTALION, THE LONDON REGIMENT.

In the Field
27th Octr. 1916.

PART 1.

1. **DETAIL** Orderly Officer   Lieut. Capes
   Orderly Sergeant   Sergt. Wilson   B.Co.

2. **ROUTINE** Reveille   6-30 a.m.   Dinners   en route
   Sick Parade   6-45 a.m.   Teas   on arrival
   Breakfast   7-0 a.m.   Orderly Room   6-0 p.m.

3. **PARADE** Reference :Map :- LENS 11 1/100,000.

   (1) The 181st Infantry Brigade will march South
   to-morrow.

   (2) The Battalion will parade at 8-30 a.m.
   Head of Column at CROSS ROADS at ETREE WARMIN
   Station and march to IVERGNY, via BEAURICOURT.

   (3) Order of March :-

          Signal Section.
          "A" Company
          "B" Company
          "C" Company
          "D" Company
          Lewis Gun Section
          Transport.

4. **GAS HELMETS** Since the arrival in the back area many men have been
   noticed walking about without Gas Helmets.
   Although it is not necessary, for safety, to wear
   them, in view of the fact that if they are nor worn many men
   will undoubtedly lose them, the Brigadier directs that the
   same shall be invariably worn, except at certain times of
   training, when it is left to the discretion of O.C.Units
   to dispense with same for the time being.

5. **DISCIPLINE** It appears that men are still carrying an unnecessarily
   large number of packages whilst on the march.
   The Brigadier directs that O.C.Units pay strict attention to this, men must not march with all sorts of extraneous
   articles tied on their packs and equipment.

PART 11.

6. **APPOINTMENT** Lieut. Colonel and Hon. Colonel F.D.Watney, Queens
   Regiment, has joined the Battalion and assumes command of it
   from to-day inclusive.

Macdonald
CAPT. & ADJUTANT
2/21st Battalion
THE LONDON REGIMENT

BATTALION ORDERS No. 18 for 29/10/16 BY COLONEL F.D.WATNEY
COMMANDING 2/21st BATTALION, THE LONDON REGIMENT
                                        In the Field
                                        28th Octr. 1916.

PART 1.

1. DETAIL   Orderly Officer   Capt. Brett
             Orderly Sergeant   Sergt. Hessey   B.Co.

2. ROUTINE   Reveille   5-30 a.m.   Dinners   on arrival
             Sick Parade 4 -0 p.m.   Teas   5-0 p.m.
             Breakfast   6 -0 a.m.   Orderly Room 4-30 p.m.

3.   Reference Map :- LENS 11 1/100,000.

3.   The 181st Infantry Brigade will continue its move South
             on the 29th inst.

4.   The Battalion will parade at 7-10 a.m. and march to
             AUTHEUX.

             Route   BARLEY - OUTREBOIS - LE QUESNEL FARM.

5.   Order of March
                         Signallers,
                         Battalion Bombers.
                         "D" Company
                         "C" Company
                         "B" Company
                         "A" Company
                         Lewis Guns.
                         Stretcher Bearers
                         Transport.

             Parade Ground   NEUVILLETTE - OCCOCHES ROAD. The
             head of the column at Battalion Q.M.Stores facing N.

                                        CAPT. ADJUTANT.
                                        2/21st Battalion,
                                        THE LONDON REGIMENT.

                    N O T I C E

        Officers valises will be at the Q.M.Stores by 6-0 a.m.
    sharp.   Mes Baskets at Battalion Headquarters at
    6-30 a.m.

WAR DIARY

BATTALION ORDERS NO. 20 for 31/10/16
                                              In the Field
                                              30th Octr. 1916.

    PART   1.

1. DETAIL   Orderly Officer   Lt. Browing
            Orderly Sergeant   Sergt. Smelt   B.Co.

2. ROUTINE Reveille   6-30 a.m.   Dinners   12-45 p.m.
            Sick Parade   6-45 a.m.   Teas   5-0 p.m.
            Breakfast   7-30 a.m.   Orderly Room 4-30 p.m.

3. PARADES 6-45 a.m. -7-15 a.m.   Parade under Platoon Commanders.
                Fatigue Dress.

           9-30 a.m. - 12-30 p.m.   Parade under Company arrangements.
                              "Attack from the Trenches".
   THE COMMANDING OFFICER WILL SEE ALL OFFICERS AT 12 NOON ON THE
           2-30 p.m.   Close Order Drill.- If wet - Lectures. (TRAINING
                                                                (GROUND.
           LEWIS GUN SECTION)   Training under their Specialist
           SIGNALLING SECTION)   Officers.

                Company Commanders will detail :-
                    12 men per Company to report at 9-30 a.m.)
                    12 men per Company to report at 2-0 p.m.)
           to Battalion Bombing Officer at Battalion Headquarters.
                Different men must be detailed each parade, in
           order that all men have practice.

           LEWIS GUN CLASS Men detailed for to-day will again parade
           under Lieut. Exall.

4. DISCIPLINE The Brigadier has noticed that in spite of previous
               orders on the subject, there is still a great deal of
               slackness on the part of N.C.Os and men paying the proper
               compliments to motor cars containing Officers which may pass
               them in the street.
                    The O.C.Battalion directs that this should be brought
               to the notice of all N.C.Os and men, and the method of
               paying proper compliments explained to them by O.C.
               Companies.

                    The following extract from General Routine Orders is
               published for the information of all ranks :-

           1886 DISCIPLINE - SLEEPING ON POST.
                    On the 25th September 1915 the Commanding-in-Chief
               had occasion to issue G.R.O. 1168 to the effect that, in
               consequence of the frequency of cases in which soldiers
               posted as sentries had been found asleep on their posts, he
               would in future be obliged to confirm sentences of death
               passed by Courts-Martial for such conduct.
                    After a period during which the Army was immune
               from this most serious and dangerous offence, it has again
               become regrettably prevalent, and the Commander-in-Chief orders
               that the troops are to be informed that if their there is any
               recurrence of this kind after the present warning, he will
               have no alternative but to carry out the extreme penalty."

(2)

5. MOVE   The following letter has been received from the Corps Commander and is circulated for the information of all ranks :

"Major General E.S.Bulfin C.V.O., C.B.
     Comdg. 60th DIVISION.

     I should be very sorry to let the Division leave the XVIIth Corps without expressing to them through you my thanks for all the hard work they have done, and my appreciation of the soldierly spirit they have shewn throughout.
     It is a great pride and pleasure to have had such a Division under one's command, and a real regret to part from them.
     I am very grateful indeed to you and your Staff for all the loyal co-operation shewn to myself and the Corps.
     I am absolutely confident that the Division will make a name for itself whenever the chance comes, and I wish you and them the best of luck and success.

           (sgd)   CHARLES FERGUSON
                           Lt. General
25/10/16.   Comdg. XVIIth Corps."

                                   Macdonald
                                 CAPT. & ADJUTANT
                                 2/21st Battalion
                                 THE LONDON REGIMENT

                   N O T I C E

     HOLY COMMUNION will be celebrated at 7 a.m. to-morrow in the barn at the rear of Battalion Headquarters.
     The Chaplain hopes that as many as possible will attend.
     All ranks to be notified.

BEF
Volume XI 181/60

Vol 6

Confidential

War Diary
of the
2/21st Battalion London Regiment

from 1/11/16 to 30/11/16

Army Form C. 2118

WAR DIARY
or
INTELLIGENCE SUMMARY
(Erase heading not required.)

2/2nd Batt. The London Regt
(R. Surrey Regt.)

Instructions regarding War Diaries and Intelligence Summaries are contained in F.S. Regs., Part II. and the Staff Manual respectively. Title Pages will be prepared in manuscript.

Place	Date	Hour	Summary of Events and Information	Remarks and references to Appendices
	1916 Nov		Reference Map. FRANCE, LENS, 11, 1/100,000. ABBEVILLE, 14, 1/100,000	
AUTHEUX	1st.		Battalion at rest. Training in preparation for SOMME carried our prosperity by Companies.	
" "	2nd.		Training continued	
" "	3rd.		Battalion marched to BERNEUIL.	Orders No. 24.
BERNEUIL	4th.		Battalion marched to VILLERS-S-AILLY.	Orders No. 25.
VILLERS	5th to 23rd		Training continued. The Battalion having received orders to proceed to SALONICA proceeded to re-equip. All damaged horses and wagons were returned and only riding horses retained. Major WRIGHT and Captain ENGLISH reported to the Base at HAVRE 23.11.16, and two subaltern officers 2/Lieut ROBERTS reported for duty 22.11.16 to complete establishment. Draft of 70 OR arrived from England 13.11.16. The training during this period consisted of close order drill, intensive digging, attack practice, and route marches. Captain WALTER took over command of B Company, and Captain EVEREST of D. 11.16	Orders No. 26
MARSEILLES	23rd		Battalion entrained for MARSEILLES	
	26th		Battalion arrived at MARSEILLES without casualty and proceeded to CARNOISSON camp, the horses being sent to FOURNIER camp.	

Army Form C. 2118

WAR DIARY
or
INTELLIGENCE SUMMARY
(Erase heading not required.)

Place	Date	Hour	Summary of Events and Information	Remarks and references to Appendices
MARSEILLES	1916 Nov 26th/27th 29th/		Battalion in CARCASSONE Camp awaiting embarkation orders.	
	30th		Battalion embarked on H.M.T INERNIA	Orders No. 49.

Helena
Major
for O in C 2/22nd London Regiment of

30/11/1916.

BATTALION ORDERS NO. 49 FOR 30/11/16 BY COL. F.D.
WATNEY, COMDG. 2/21st BATTALION, LONDON REGT.

In the Field
29th Novr. 1916
PART 1.

1. DETAIL Orderly Officer   2/Lt. ANTROBUS
          Orderly Sergeant   L/Sgt. WRIGHTON   A.Co.
          Orderly Corporal   L/Cpl. DUNFORD   A.Co.

2. ROUTINE   Reveille   4-30 a.m.
                Breakfast   5-15 a.m.

3. PARADES 6-0 a.m.   Advance Parties, as elsewhere
                      detailed, parade at times as
                      stated below.

         The Battalion will parade ready
   to move off at times as under :-
         "D" Company   7-0 a.m.
         "C"   "   7-15 a.m.
         "B"   "   7-30 a.m.
         "A"   "   7-45 a.m.
         Companies will move off at
   above mentioned times.   Haversack
   ration to be carried.

   BLANKETS   rolled in bundles of 10 and
   securely tied, to be at end of Company
   lines by 5-15 a.m..

   TENTS   cleaned by 6-30 a.m.

   ADVANCE PARTIES will parade ready to move
   at times as under :-
   6-0 a.m.   20 men and 2 N.C.Os of "A" Co.
                        under 2/Lt. SMITH.
   6-10 a.m. (50 men & 6 N.C.Os of "B") under
             (50 men & 6 N.C.Os of "A") 2/Lts.
                                HAMILTON & MARTIN.

   Garfield Macdonald
                              Capt & Adjt. 2/21LR

SECRET

BATTALION MOVE ORDERS NO. 26 for 23/11/16
In the Field
22nd Novr. 1916

Reference Maps :- LENS (11))
ABBEVILLE (14)) 1/100,000

1. The Battalion will march to LONGPRE Station to-morrow, to entrain.

2. ROUTE   LONG - LE CATELOT - LONGPRE Station

3. ORDER OF MARCH

    Advanced Guard   (2 Platoons of "A" Compy.
                         under Capt. BLOY)
    "A" Company   (less 2 Platoons)
    "B" do
    "C" do
    "D" do   (less 1 Platoon)
    Stretcher Bearers
    Transport
    Rear Guard   (1 Platoon "D" Company
                         & Regimental Police.

Copy No. 1 C.O.
     "   2 O.C. A.Co.
     "   3 O.C. B.Co.
     "   4 O.C. C.Co.
     "   5 O.C. D.Co.
     "   6 M.O.
     "   7 Q.M.
     "   8 S.O.
     "   9 R.D.

CAPT. & ADJUTANT
2/21st Battalion,
THE LONDON REGIMENT

BATTALION MOVE ORDERS No. 25 for 4/11/16

In the Field
3rd Novr. 1916.

Ref. Map :- LENS 11 1/100,000

(1) The Battalion will move to-morrow to VILLERS-SOUS-AILLY.

(2) <u>ROUTE</u> BERNEUIL - DOMART-EN-PONTHIEU - VAUCHELLES-LES-DOMART.

(3) <u>PARADE</u> ready to move at 9-10 a.m. on the BERNEUIL - DOMART-EN-PONTHIEU Road. Head of Column outside Battalion Headquarters.

(4) <u>DRESS</u> Full Marching Order.

(5) <u>ORDER OF MARCH</u> Signallers, Bombers, Band, "C" Co., "B" Co., "A" Co., "D" Co., (less 1 Platoon), Lewis Gunners, Stretcher Bearers, Transport, 1 Platoon "D" Company.

Issued at 4 p.m. 3/11/16.

1Copy to 181st Inf. Bde.

Copies to all Officers concerned.

CAPT. & ADJUTANT
2/21st Battalion,
THE LONDON REGIMENT.

BATTALION MOVE ORDERS No. 24 for 3/11/16. WAR DIARY

                                          In the Field
                                          2nd Novr. 1916.

Ref. Map :-   LENS 11 1/100,000

(1)   The Battalion will move to-morrow to BERNEUIL via
       FIENVILLERS

(2) <u>PARADE</u>   Battalion Alarm Post at 9-45 a.m.

(3) <u>DRESS</u>   Full Marching Order.

(4) <u>ORDER OF MARCH</u>   Signallers,   Bombers,   Band,
       "D" Co.,   "C" Co.,   "B" Co.,   "A" Co., (less
       1 Platoon),   Lewis Gunners,   Stretcher Bearers,
       Transport,   1 Platoon "A" Company.

Issued at 7-45 p.m. 2/11/16.

1 Copy to 181st Inf. Bde.   CAPT. & ADJUTANT
Copies to all Officers concerned.   2/21st Batt. LOND. REGT.

60 DIVISION

181 BRIGADE

2/21 LONDON REGT

1915 OCT — 1916 MAY

2904

Army Form C. 2118.

WAR DIARY
or
INTELLIGENCE SUMMARY.

Hockerill Camp,
Bishops Stortford,
2nd. October 1915.

2/21 LON

(Erase heading not required.)

Instructions regarding War Diaries and Intelligence Summaries are contained in F. S. Regs., Part II. and the Staff Manual respectively. Title pages will be prepared in manuscript.

Place	Date	Hour	Summary of Events and Information	Remarks and references to Appendices
Hockerill and neighbourhood			Physical Training, Company, Battalion & Brigade Training, Night operations, Musketry Instruction.	
Hadham Park			Trench digging	
Trenching Ground			" " by night.	
			Bomb throwing instruction (2 Officers 22 other ranks)	
Bishops Stortford and neighbourhood			Field cooking.	

H. S. Cobbold.
Colonel,
Commanding 2/21st. Batt. London Regt.

1577 Wt.W10791/1773 500,000 1/15 D. D. & L. A.D.S.S./Forms/C. 2118.

Army Form C. 2118.

A

WAR DIARY
or
INTELLIGENCE-SUMMARY.
(Erase heading not required.)

Coggeshall
Essex.
3rd. Novr. 1915.

Instructions regarding War Diaries and Intelligence Summaries are contained in F. S. Regs., Part II. and the Staff Manual respectively. Title pages will be prepared in manuscript.

Place	Date	Hour	Summary of Events and Information	Remarks and references to Appendices
Hockerill Camp and neighbourhood.			Physical Training, Company, Battalion and Brigade Training	
Braintree Dunmow			Musketry Instruction, Night operations.	
			Manoeuvres	
			Alarm Practice. Air raids.	
Hadham Park			Bombing. Throwing Instruction.	
			Trench Digging	
Bishops Stortford Dunmow Coggeshall	1st. & 2nd. Novr.		Move from Camp at Hockerill to Billets at Coggeshall.	

H.F. Colbrott.
Colonel
Comdg. 2/21st. Battn., London Regt.

1577 Wt.W10791/1773 500,000 1/15 D.D.& L. A.D.S.S./Forms/C. 2118.

Army Form C. 2118.

WAR DIARY
or
INTELLIGENCE SUMMARY.
(Erase heading not required.)

REF. MAP. ORDNANCE SURVEY SHEET 30.
½" = 1 MILE.

Instructions regarding War Diaries and Intelligence Summaries are contained in F. S. Regs., Part II. and the Staff Manual respectively. Title pages will be prepared in manuscript.

Place	Date	Hour	Summary of Events and Information	Remarks and references to Appendices
HOCKERILL	1/11/15	9.45am	Battalion proceeded by route march to GREAT DUNMOW.	1/21 Zaps
GREAT DUNMOW	2/11/15	9 am	Battalion proceeded by route march to COGGESHALL, ESSEX viâ BRAINTREE	1/21 Zaps
COGGESHALL	3/11/15 to 10/11/15		Battalion training adjacent to Billets in Physical drill, Bayonet fighting, bombing close order drill etc..	1/21 Zaps
do.	11/11/15	2pm	Inspection of Billets by G.O.C 60th (LONDON) DIVISION.	1/21 Zaps
do	11/11/15	6pm	Villages of SIBYL HEDINGHAM and CASTLE HEDINGHAM placed out of bounds owing to Typhoid Fever	1/21 Zaps
do	13/11/15	12 noon	Japanese .256 Rifles & Bayonets withdrawn from men for despatch to WEEDON	1/21 Zaps
do	14/11/15	10am	.303 Short Rifles & 159,750 rounds Mk.VI .303 ammunition received from WEEDON.	1/21 Zaps
do	19/11/15	4pm	104,240 rounds Japanese ammunition & Japanese rifles & Bayonets despatched to WEEDON	1/21 Zaps
do	27/11/15	11am	Inspection of Books by COL. COMMANDING 181ST INFANTRY BRIGADE	1/21 Zaps
do	30/11/15	10am	2/Lieuts TEAROE, BROWNING, EXALL, NEARY, proceeded to join the 3/21st BATTN. LONDON REGIMENT at CARSHALTON.	1/21 Zaps

H.S.Oldfield. Col.
Comdg. 1/21st Batt. London Rgt.

VOLUME 1.

WAR DIARY

of the

2/21st BATTALION, THE LONDON REGIMENT

from

1st DECEMBER 1915 to 31st DECEMBER 1915.

CONFIDENTIAL

WAR DIARY or INTELLIGENCE SUMMARY.

Army Form C. 2118.

Place	Date	Hour	Summary of Events and Information	Remarks and references to Appendices
COGGESHALL	1/12/15	9 a.m.	Company Training	JMS
"	2/12/15	8-25 a.m.	Brigade Exercise at ABBOTTS HALL. Distance marched by Battalion in full marching order. 22 miles (approximately) No Casualties.	JMS
"	3/12/15	9 a.m.	Battalion Exercise at GREAT TEY cancelled owing to weather conditions, and barrack room instruction in Outposts substituted.	JMS
"	4/12/15	9 a.m.	Physical Drill and Bayonet Fighting.	JMS
"	"	11 a.m.	Interior Economy.	JMS
"	5/12/15	9-40 a.m.	Church Parade.	JMS
"	6/12/15	8-55 a.m.	Company Training	JMS
"	7/12/15	8-55 a.m.	Company Training	JMS
"	8/12/15	8-55 a.m.	Company Training	JMS
"	9/12/15	9 a.m	ditto	JMS
"	10/12/15	9 a.m.	Battalion Outpost Scheme at GREAT TEY.	See Appendix A.
"	10/12/15		Lt. Col. & Hon. Col H.S Coldicott V.D. transferred to Command 3rd Line Depot (Authority :- London District Order No. 14, dated 7th December 1915). MAJOR B. COLDICOTT FLETCHER assumes Command of the Battalion.	JMS

Army Form C. 2118.

WAR DIARY
or
INTELLIGENCE SUMMARY.
(Erase heading not required.)

Instructions regarding War Diaries and Intelligence Summaries are contained in F.S. Regs., Part II. and the Staff Manual respectively. Title pages will be prepared in manuscript.

Place	Date	Hour	Summary of Events and Information	Remarks and references to Appendices
	1915			
COGGESHALL	11/12	9 a.m.	Company Training. Interior Economy.	Ars
"	12/12	9-10 a.m.	Church Parade.	Ars
"	13/12	9 a.m.	Company Training.	Ars
"	14/12	9 a.m.	Company Training.	Ars
"	15/12	8-55 a.m.	Company Training.	Ars
"	16/12	9 a.m.	Route March via EARLS COLNE - WAKES COLNE - FORDHAM - MARKS TEY. Short distance covered 16 miles. Dress :- Marching Order. One casualty.	Ars
"	17/12	9 a.m.	Tactical Exercise at MARKS HALL.	See Appendix B.
"	18/12	9 a.m.	Company Training. Interior Economy.	Ars
"	18/12		CAPTAINS S.H.TEUTEN & H.R.S.COLDICOTT & 2/LIEUTS F.G.BARRETT & S.A.F.NEARY transferred to 3rd LINE DEPOT. (Authority C.F.letter 10697 (A) dated 14/12/15)	Ars
"	19/12	9-40 a.m.	Church Parade.	Ars
"	20/12	9 a.m.	Company Training.	Ars
"	21/12	9 a.m.	Company Training.	Ars
"	22/12	6-30 a.m.	Battalion turned out on "ALARM" and were ready to march from Battalion Alarm Post at 9-35 a.m. All billets cleared, and necessary stores loaded.	See Appendix C.

1577 Wt.W10791/1773 500,000 1/15 D.D.&L. A.D.S.S./Forms/C. 2118.

Army Form C. 2118.

WAR DIARY
or
INTELLIGENCE SUMMARY.
(Erase heading not required.)

Instructions regarding War Diaries and Intelligence Summaries are contained in F. S. Regs., Part II. and the Staff Manual respectively. Title pages will be prepared in manuscript.

Place	Date	Hour	Summary of Events and Information	Remarks and references to Appendices
	1915			
COGGESHALL	22/12	9-35 a.m.	March to STISTED commenced but cancelled owing to weather conditions.	JW
"	"	11 a.m.	Battalion Drill.	JW
"	"		GOSFIELD placed out of bounds owing to infectious disease. (Authority :- 60th (London) Divisional Order 355, dated 20/12/15)	JW
"	23/12	9 a.m.	Physical Drill & Bayonet Fighting.	JW
"	"	11 a.m.	Battalion Drill.	JW
"	"	2-30 p.m.	Inspection by G.O.C. 60th (London) Division.	JW
"	24/12	9 a.m.	Company Training.	JW
"	25/12		Christmas Day. General leave. Message from H.M. the KING published for information of all ranks.	See Appendix D. JW
"	26/12	9-40 a.m.	Church Parade.	JW
"	27/12		General leave.	JW
"	28/12	9 a.m.	Company Training.	JW
"	29/12/15	9 a.m.	Company Training.	JW
"		10 a.m.	MAJOR B. FLETCHER proceeded to FRANCE to be temporarily attached to the ARMY in the FIELD (Authority :- 60th (London) Divisional Order No. 360 dated 28/12/15)	JW

Army Form C. 2118.

WAR DIARY
or
INTELLIGENCE SUMMARY.
(Erase heading not required.)

Instructions regarding War Diaries and Intelligence Summaries are contained in F. S. Regs., Part II. and the Staff Manual respectively. Title pages will be prepared in manuscript.

Place	Date	Hour	Summary of Events and Information	Remarks and references to Appendices
	1915			
COGGESHALL	29/12	10 a.m.	MAJOR S. WRIGHT assumes Command of the Battalion.	JWS
"	30/12	8-45 a.m.	Brigade exercise at GOSFIELD HALL PARK. Approximate distance covered 20 miles.	See Appendix E. JWS
			Dress :- Marching Order. Five Casualties.	See Appendix F. JWS
"	31/12	9 a.m.	Battalion exercise at GREAT TEY.	

S Wright
Major
OC. 2/21st Battn London Regiment

APPENDIX A.

181st INFANTRY BRIGADE TACTICAL EXERCISE - 10 DECEMBER 1915.

(continuation of Tactical Exercise of 26th November 1915).

BATTALION ORDERS OF COLONEL H.S. COLDICOTT V.D.
COMMANDING 2/21st BATTALION, THE LONDON REGIMENT.

Ref. O.S. Sheet 98. 1" - 1 mile.   MARKS HALL
                                    10/12/15

1. The enemy - reported to be short of supplies - has withdrawn his advanced troops from ALDHAM.
Our Main Body moves from STISTED to-day and bivouacs at MARKS HALL.
The 181st Infantry Brigade has been ordered to occupy an advanced outpost line CHAPEL - GREAT TEY - LITTLE TEY.

2. The 2/21st Battalion will be responsible for the section of the line from point 225 to GREAT TEY Church inclusive. Its flank will be secured by other troops from the Brigade.

3. The Battalion will be distributed as per margin.

Outpost Coys

"A" Coy.   Frontage of "A" Company from point 225 to Smithy inclusive.
"D" Coy.   "C" Company from Smithy exclusive to G in GREAT TEY
"D" Coy.   "D" Company from G in GREAT TEY to Church inclusive.
 Reserve
"B" Coy.   Reserve at TEY CROSS.

Troops will be in position by 11 a.m. to-day.

4. Reports to TEY CROSS.

CAPT. & ADJUTANT
2/21st Battalion,
THE LONDON REGIMENT.

Issued at 7 a.m.

No. 1 copy to 181st Infantry Brigade.
 " 2   "   " "A" Company
 " 3   "   " "B"   "
 " 4   "   " "C"   "
 " 5   "   " "D"   "
 " 6   "   Retained.

Appendix **B**

17th December 1915

181st INFANTRY BRIGADE TACTICAL EXERCISE

BATTALION ORDERS BY MAJOR B. FLETCHER

COMMANDING 2/21st BATTALION, THE LONDON REGIMENT

Ref. O.S. Sheet 98   1" - 1 mile.

COGGESHALL
17/12/15.

1.	The enemy has landed in the neighbourhood of CLACTON-ON-SEA. His advanced troops are reported about ALDHAM. Our main body if at STISTED. The 181st Infantry Brigade has been ordered to occupy an outpost line BURTONS GREEN - MARKS HALL - HOLFIELD GRANGE.
2.	The 2/21st Battalion will be responsible for the section of the line from a point about 200 yards W. of P in DEER PARK to the S.E. corner of BUNGATE WOOD. Each flank will be secured by other troops from the Brigade.
3.	The distribution will be as per margin.
Outpost Coys	
"A" Coy.	"A" Company will occupy a frontage from the S.E. corner of BUNGATE WOOD - near the E in BUNGATE to point 165.
"B" Coy.	"B" Company from Point 165 to a point 200 yards N. of K in MARKSWELL.
"C" Coy.	"C" Coy. from last names point to a point about 200 yards W. of P in DEER PARK.
4. Reserve	
"D" Coy.	"D" Company will be in reserve in GREAT MONKS WOOD. Troops will be in position by 11 a.m. to-day.
5.	Reports to Reserve.

CAPT. & ADJUTANT.
2/21st Battalion,
THE LONDON REGIMENT.

Issued at 7 a.m.

No. 1 copy to 181st Infantry Brigade by Motor Cyclist
" 2 "   " "A" Company)
" 3 "   " "B"   "   )
" 4 "   " "C"   "   ) by Orderly
" 5 "   " "D"   "   )

Appendix **C**

Copy No 6.

Order No 1.

181st INFANTRY BRIGADE

SECRET

PART 1

1. A concentration of the 181st Brigade (less 2/22nd. Battn London Regiment) will take place on Tuesday 21/12/15.

2. Composition of Brigade:-

   Commanding   Col. C.N. Watts.

   Staff Officers   Brigade Staff

   Troops   Sect. 60th Div.Sig.Co:R.E.
                        181st Infantry Brigade.
                        (less 2/22nd Bn.Ln.Regt)
                        181st Coy. A.S.C.,
                        2/6th Lndn. Field Ambulance.

3. The Position of the Assembly will be STISTED PARK.

4. Units will commence mobilizing immediately on receipt of order "Concentrate".

5. Alarm Orders will be acted on so far as they are not modified by Appendix 1.

Copy 6

181st Brigade Order No 2

Ref.½" Map Sheet
30.
                                                CLOCK TOWER.
                                                BRAINTREE.

1. The Brigade (less 2/22nd Battn Lndn Regt) will concentrate at Stisted Park at 11.30 am.
2. The starting point will be Road Junction immediately West of the "B" in Braintree.

Advanced Guard
Commander:-
Major. H.Dowsbury
Troops 2 Companies
2/24th Battn.Lndn.Rgt

3. The advanced Guard (Troops as per margin) will be clear of the Starting point by 9.50 am

Main Body
Brigade HQrs.
Sect.60th.Div.Sig.
Co.R.E.
2/24th Bn.(less 2
Coys) Brigade Machine
Guns 2/23rd Bn.LndnRgt
(less 1 platoon)
2/6th Lon.Fld.Amb.
Brigade Train
181st Coy A.S.C.

4. The Head of the Main Body (order of march as per per margin) will pass the starting point at 10 am.

5. Route BRAINTREE-JENKINS FARM-MILL-WESTLODGE, STISTED PARK.
6. The 2/21st Battn.London Regt.will concentrate independently.

Rear Guard
Commander detailed
by O.C. 2/23rd.Bn.Ln
Rgt.
1 Platoon 2/23rd
Bn.Ln.Regt.,

7. Units Trains(less 2/21st Battn.Lndn Rgt. in order of march of Units will be Brigaded under the command of Lieut. Dunn, 2/24th Battn.Lndn.Rgt.,

8. Reports to Head of Main Body

After arrival at Position of Assembly to Brigade Headquarters, STISTED PARK.

                (signed) J.N.Horlick,
                        Captain,
                        Brigade Major,
                        181st Infantry Brigade.

Issued at
By
Copy No 1 Filed
Copy No 2 to 60th Divn by post 20/12/15.
Copy No 4 to O.C. Brigade Machine Gun by Orderly
Copy No 3 to O.C.Sect 60th Divl Sig.Co R.E. by Orderly
Copy No 5 to OC. Brigade Train by Orderly
Copy No 6 to O.C. 2/21st Bn.London Regt by cycle Orderly
Copy No 7 to O.C. 2/23rd Bn. Regt.   )
Copy No 8 to O.C. 2/24th Ban.Lndn Regt   )
Copy No 9 to O.C. 181st Coy A.S.C.   ) By Orderly
Copy No 10 to O.C.2/6th Lon.Field Ambulance)

APPENDIX D

SPECIAL ORDER BY MAJOR B. FLETCHER, COMMANDING 2/21st
BATTALION, THE LONDON REGIMENT.

COGGESHALL.
25th Decr. 1915.

EXTRACT. The following extract from 60th (London) Division Special Order, dated 24th Decr. 1915, is published for the information of all ranks :-

"The following gracious message has been received from H.M. THE KING, and is, by his command, re-published for the information of all ranks in Orders at the various Garrison Towns, Defensible Ports, and Military Camps on Christmas Day :-

"Another Christmas finds all the resources
"of the Empire still engaged in War, and I desire
"to convey, on my own behalf and on behalf of the
"Queen, a heartfelt Christmas greeting and our good
"wishes for the New Year to all who, on sea and
"land, are upholding the honour of the British name.
"In the Officers and men of my Navy, on whom
"the security of the Empire depends, I repose, in
"common with all my subjects, a trust that is
"absolute.
"On the Officers and men of my Armies, whether
"now in France, in the East, or in other fields, I
"rely with an equal faith, confident that their
"devotion, their valour, and their self-sacrifice
"will, under God's guidance, lead to victory and an
" honourable peace.
"There are many of their comrades now, alas,
"in hospital, and to these brave men also I desire,
"with the Queen, to express our deep gratitude and
"our earnest prayers for their recovery.
"Officers and men of the Navy and Army,
"another year is drawing to a close as it began, in
"toil, bloodshed and suffering, but I rejoice to
"know that the goal to which you are striving
"draws nearer into sight.
"May God bless you and all your undertakings"

The G.O.C. permits Monday, 27th December 1915, to be observed as a holiday at the discretion of Officers Commanding Brigades and Divisional Troops.

CAPT. & ADJUTANT.
2/21st Battalion,
THE LONDON REGIMENT.

APPENDIX E

GENERAL IDEA

Reference O.S. ½" No. 30, and any map of Eastern Counties.

KHAKI Home Defence Troops are moving Northwards to the line CAMBRIDGE - IPSWICH to resist the advance on LONDON of a GREY invading force, which has landed on the NORFOLK COAST.

SPECIAL IDEA -------- KHAKI FORCE

The 60th (London) Division is ordered to concentrate at HAVERHILL on the COLCHESTER - CAMBRIDGE Branch Line of the G.E.Railway.

Copy No. 3

181st INFANTRY BRIGADE Order No. 1

BRAINTREE
29th December 1915.

Reference O.S. ½" No. 30
& any map of Eastern
Counties.

1. (a) A Grey Invading Force which has landed on the NORFOLK COAST is moving on LONDON.
   (b) The 60th (London) Division is ordered to concentrate at HAVERHILL as part of a movement of Home Defence Troops to resist the enemy's advance.
2. The 181st Infantry Brigade (less the 2/22nd Battalion, London Regiment) will concentrate at GOSFIELD PARK to-morrow en route to HAVERHILL. Rendezvous Eastern Entrance of the Park.
3. The 2/22nd Battalion, London Regiment will stand fast at DUNMOW with special orders (imaginary)
4. The 2/21st Battalion, London Regiment will march at 8-45 a.m. and follow the route COGGESHALL, HOVELS FARM, TUMBLERS GREEN, STISTED RECTORY, BOULTWOODS FARM, ROMAN ROAD.
5. The Troops in BRAINTREE will march at 10 a.m. at which hour the head of the main body will pass the Starting point.
6. Starting point The MILL in BOCKING.
7. Advanced Guard, composition as in margin.

Advanced Guard
Commander Major Dicks.
2/23rd Lond. Regt.
Signal Section R.E.
One Company 2/23rd Lond. Regt.

Order of March
Brigade Machine Guns
2/23rd Lond. Regt.
(less one Company)
2/24th Lond. Regt.
Eschelon B. First Line Transport under command of Senior Transport Officer.
No. 6 Field Ambulance
Battn. Trains in order of march of Units
181st Brigade Coy. A.S.C.
The trains and the A.S.C. under command of O.C. A.S.C.

8. Main body, order of march as in the margin.

9. Reports to head of main body.
10. Further orders will be issued at the rendezvous.

(Sgd) J.N. HORLICK
Captain
Brigade Major,
181st Infantry Brigade.

Issued at   a.m.
Copy No. 1 filed
"   No. 2 Divl. H.Q.
"   No. 3 2/21st Batt. Lond. Regt.
"   No. 4 2/22nd Batt. Lond. Regt.
"   No. 5 2/23rd Batt. Lond. Regt.
"   No. 6 2/24th Batt. Lond. Regt.
"   No. 7 O.C. 2/6th Field Ambulance.
"   No. 8 181st Coy. A.S.C.
"   No. 9 O.C. Sig. Coy. R.E.

APPENDIX F.

181st INFANTRY BRIGADE TACTICAL EXERCISE 31st DECEMBER 1915

BATTALION ORDERS OF MAJOR S. WRIGHT
COMMANDING 2/21st BATTALION, THE LONDON REGIMENT.

Ref. O.S.Sheet 98. 1" - 1 mile   MARKS HALL
                                                       31/12/15

1. The enemy is reported in the neighbourhood of ALDHAM.
   Our Main Body is in bivouac at MARKS HALL.
   The 181st Infantry Brigade has been ordered to occupy an advanced outpost line CHAPEL - GREAT TEY - LITTLE TEY.

2. The 2/21st Battalion, will be responsible for the section of the line from point 225 to GREAT TEY Church inclusive. Its flank will be secured by other troops from the Brigade.

3. The Battalion will be distributed as per margin.

   <u>Outpost Coys.</u>
   "C" Coy.   Frontage of "C" Company from point 225 to Smithy inclusive.
   "D" Coy.   "D" Company from Smithy exclusive to G in GREAT TEY.
   "B" Coy.   "B" Company from G in <u>GREAT TEY</u> to Church Inclusive

   <u>Reserve</u>
   "A" Coy.   Reserve at TEY CROSS.

   Troops will be in position by 11 a.m. to-day.

4. Reports to TEY CROSS.

                                           [signature]
                                           CAPT. & ADJUTANT
                                           2/21st Battalion,
Issued at 7 a.m.   THE LONDON REGIMENT.

No. 1 copy to 181st Infantry Brigade by motor cyclist
 " 2 "   " "A" Company by orderly.
 " 3 "   " "B"   "   "   "
 " 4 "   " "C"   "   "   "
 " 5 "   " "D"   "   "   "
 " 6 "   retained.

Volume II. Number I.

County of London Battalion Orderly Room — First Surrey Rifles — London Regiment

War Diary

of the

2/21st Battn. The London Regt.

January 1st to 31st 1916.

Confidential

Army Form C. 2118.

WAR DIARY
or
INTELLIGENCE SUMMARY.
(Erase heading not required.)

Instructions regarding War Diaries and Intelligence Summaries are contained in F.S. Regs., Part II. and the Staff Manual respectively. Title pages will be prepared in manuscript.

Place	Date	Hour	Summary of Events and Information	Remarks and references to Appendices
	1916			
COGGESHALL	1st Jan	9 a.m.	Physical drill bayonet fighting etc	AGT.
"	"	11 a.m.	Interior Economy.	AGT.
"	2nd Jan	9.40 a.m.	Church Parade	AGT.
"	3rd Jan	9 a.m.	Company Training	AGT.
"	4th Jan	9 a.m.	Route march. Route taken KELVEDON – MESSING – MARKS TEY – COGGESHALL Distance = 14 miles. Number of casualties nil. Roads were in a very bad condition owing to recent floods.	AGT.
"	5th Jan	9 a.m.	Company Training. Training of snipers organised.	See Appendix I
"	"	11 a.m.	Inspection of company conduct sheets by Lt Col Nash LIEUT-COL. NASH	
"	"	"	Inspection of horses by COL. LANE A.V.C. of 60th (LONDON) DIVISION. Number of horses cast as unfit for military service	
"	"	"	MAJOR B. FLETCHER assumes command of the Battalion vice MAJOR S. WRIGHT.	AGT.
"	"	2.30 p.m.	War Office Confidential letter No. 80/919 (M.O.5) dated 12th December 1915 received	
"	"	"	War Office letter No 9/GEN NO:/5757 (M.T.2) dated 23rd December and Syllabus of training received	AGT.
"	6th Jan	9 a.m.	Company training LIEUT. A.C. TEUTON proceeded to course of instruction at ONGAR. (Field Engineering etc)	AGT.

1577 Wt.W10791/1773 500,000 1/15 D.D.&L. A.D.S.S./Forms/C. 2118.

Army Form C. 2118.

WAR DIARY
or
INTELLIGENCE SUMMARY.
(Erase heading not required.)

Instructions regarding War Diaries and Intelligence Summaries are contained in F.S. Regs., Part II. and the Staff Manual respectively. Title pages will be prepared in manuscript.

Place	Date	Hour	Summary of Events and Information	Remarks and references to Appendices
COGGESHALL	1916. 7th Jan	9 a.m.	Battalion tactical exercise S.E. of EARLS COLNE	See Appendix II
	8th	9 a.m.	Company training	
		11 a.m.	Interior economy	
	9th Jan	9.40 a.m.	Church Parade	
	10th	9 a.m.	Route march combined with tactical scheme	See Appendix III
	11th	9 a.m.	Company training	
		6 p.m.	Orders received to fill in instructional trenches preparatory to move.	
	12th Jan	9 a.m.	All companies filling in trenches and clearing ground at MARKS HALL etc	
	13th Jan	9 a.m.	All companies filling in trenches and clearing ground at MARKS HALL etc.	
		5 p.m.	Draft of 350 men received from 3rd LINE DEPOT. CAPT. H.A. MILTON and LIEUT W.J.A. UNDERWOOD transferred to 2/23RD BATTN. LONDON REGT. (Auth. L.D Orders & para 17 dated 10/1/16)	
	14th Jan	9 a.m.	Route march under REGIMENTAL SERGEANT MAJOR. All officers attended lecture at HEADQUARTERS 181st INFANTRY BRIGADE by MAJOR R.B. CAMPBELL on PHYSICAL EXERCISES and BAYONET FIGHTING.	
		2.30 p.m.	DRAFT inspected by COL. C.N. WATTS COMMANDING 181ST INFANTRY BRIGADE.	
	15th Jan	9 a.m.	Company training	
		11 a.m.	Interior economy	

Army Form C. 2118.

WAR DIARY
or
INTELLIGENCE SUMMARY.
(Erase heading not required.)

Instructions regarding War Diaries and Intelligence Summaries are contained in F. S. Regs., Part II. and the Staff Manual respectively. Title pages will be prepared in manuscript.

Place	Date	Hour	Summary of Events and Information	Remarks and references to Appendices
	1916			
COGGESHALL	16th Jan	9:40 a.m.	Church Parade.	A/S
	17th Jan	9 a.m.	All companies filling in trenches at MARKS HALL. Examination of officers for promotion by COL: C.N. WATTS. COMMANDING 181ST INFANTRY BRIGADE.	A/S
	18th Jan	9 a.m.	All companies filling in trenches at MARKS HALL. CAPTAIN R.S.H. COLDICOTT. 2"LIEUT F. BARRATT and 2"LIEUT NEARY transferred from 3rd LINE DEPOT. LIEUT. V.R. FLETCHER is seconded for duty with a PROVISIONAL BATTALION (Authority LONDON DISTRICT ORDERS No. 12 dated 14th Jan 1916)	A/S See Appendix IV
	19th Jan	9 a.m.	Tactical exercise at FEERING.	
	20th Jan	9 a.m.	Company training	
		11:30 a.m.	Inspection of draft by G.O.C. 60th (LONDON) DIVISION. (Owing to rain actual inspection was at 12:15 p.m.)	A/S
	21st Jan	9 a.m.	Company training. All troops preparing for move.	
	22nd Jan	10 a.m.	Advanced party under command 2"LIEUT. R. BRETT entrains for SUTTON VENY.	A/S
	23rd Jan	9:40 a.m.	Battalion Colours Battalion preparing to move to SUTTON VENY.	A/S
	24th Jan	12:15 a.m.	"C" & "D" Companies parade to move to SUTTON VENY. Arrived WARMINSTER 8:33am	
		? 2 a.m.	"A" & "B" Companies parade to move to SUTTON VENY. Arrived WARMINSTER 10 a.m.	A/S
	25th Jan	8:30	Battalion parade in fatigue dress.	
	26th Jan	8:30	Battalion parade in fatigue dress. Latest recruits & medically unfit men inspected by GENERAL THE RT HON. SIR A.H. PAGET G.C.B., K.C.V.O.	A/S

Army Form C. 2118.

WAR DIARY
or
INTELLIGENCE SUMMARY.
(Erase heading not required.)

Instructions regarding War Diaries and Intelligence Summaries are contained in F. S. Regs., Part II. and the Staff Manual respectively. Title pages will be prepared in manuscript.

Place	Date	Hour	Summary of Events and Information	Remarks and references to Appendices
SUTTON VENY	1916			
	27th Jan	9 am	Brigade route march. Route :- Camp W entrance to SUTTON VENY - LONGBRIDGE DEVERAL to 1st Nm	
"	28th Jan	11 am	HORNINGSHAM thence to Pt E of NEWBURY to S fork roads 1/2 mile W of R in Casualties :- One.	Apt
		8.30 am	REFORMATORY thence to COCKERTON - COCKERTON GREEN to GREEN HILLS & CAMP.	
			Inspection of lines by G.O.C. 60th (LONDON) DIVISION	
	29th Jan	8.30 am	Battalion parade in fatigue dress. Interior economy etc	Apt
	30th Jan	9 am	Church Parade	Apt
"	31st Jan	9 am	Brigade Parade to practice for W Inspection	
		1.30	at	
		3 pm		
"		6 pm	War Office secret document No 366 :- "Notes on employment of machine guns received." Apt	
	31st Jan	7.30 am	Squad drill.	
		11.40 am	Battalion Parade for Inspection by FIELD MARSHALL LORD FRENCH. INSPECTOR	Apt
			GENERAL OF HOME DEFENCE FORCES.	

J.J. Fletcher
Lt. Colonel
O.C. 2/21st Battn London Regt.

APPENDIX. I

PROGRAMME OF TRAINING
SNIPERS.

———o———

Advanced Musketry Course:-
   1st Week

      (a) Care of Arms and mechanism   Sgt.Major Prince

      (b) Theory of rifle fire   2/Lt. Reynolds

      (c) Visual training and judging distance   Lieut.Macdonald.

      (d) Use of Cover, ground etc.   Capt.Walter

   2nd week

      (a) Reconnaissance and reports)
      (b) Map reading   )
) Capt. Walter.
      (c) Compass and binoculars   )
      (d) Night Work   )

   3rd week

      (a) Construction of loopholes and observation posts   Capt Everest

      (b) Use of Periscope

   4th week

      (a) Use of Range finding instruments   2/ Lt.Reynolds

      (b) Observation of fire   Capt Walter & Lt.Macdonald

Practical Work in minature range to run concurrently under Musketry Instructors detailed.

+++++++++++++++

APPENDIX II

BRIGADE EXERCISE   7th JANUARY 1916

<u>BATTALION ORDERS BY MAJOR B.FLETCHER</u>

<u>COMMANDING THE</u>

<u>2/21st BATTALION, THE LONDON REGIMENT.</u>

Ref.Ord.Survey.   Hains Farm,
   Sheet 98 1"=1 mile.   7/1/16.

<u>Outpost Coys.</u>
  <u>A.Coy</u>
From BURNT HOUSE
FARM TO BALDWINS
FARM inclusive.
  <u>B.Coy</u>
From BALDWINS
FARM due S. to
200 CONTOUR.
  <u>D.Coy</u>
From 200 CONTOUR
to PALMERS FARM
inclusive.
  <u>Reserve</u>
  <u>C.Coy</u>
AT MITCHELLS FARM.

1. The enemy is advancing W. from LAYER DE LA HAYE. His advanced troops are reported at COPFORD. Our main Force is in bivouac at HAINS FARM.
2. The 2/21st Battalion will occupy advanced outpost position from PALMERS FARM to BURNT HOUSE FARM.
3. Distribution will be as per margin.

   Troops to be in position by 11 am.

4. Reports to MITCHELLS FARM.

                                    Captain and Adjutant,
                                     2/21st Battalion,
                                      London Regiment.

Issued at 9 am

Copy No 1   181st Brigade by Motor Cyclist.
  "   " 2   O.C. A.Coy
  "   " 3   " B.Coy
  "   " 4   " C.Coy
  "   " 5   " D.Coy
  "   " 6   Retained.

Appendix III

GENERAL IDEA

Ref.Ord.Sur. 98)
  1"=1 mile   )

Whiteland and Brownland are at war. The
boundary between the two countries being
ROMAN RIVER

SPECIAL IDEA

Message received at Kelvedon at 9.45 am:-
O.C.2/21st Battn. London Regiment, KELVEDON AAA.
Small enemy raiding force reported to have
crossed frontier about WALCOTTS FARM at
8.30am today AAA objective believed to be
COGGESHALL AAA. March at once as strong as
possible intercept and drive beyond frontier.
AAA.   O.C. BROWN FORCE

++++++++++++

APPENDIX IV

SCHEME FOR NIGHT OPERATIONS 19/1/16.

GENERAL IDEA

A Khaki force is holding an entrenched line MARKS TEY -WITHAM facing south east.

SPECIAL IDEA

The 181st Infantry Brigade hold the sector of the line from D. of ROMAN ROAD to R of ROMAN with the 2/23rd and 2/24th Battalions, London Regiment in the trenches 2/21st and 2/22nd Battalions in reserve.

The 2/21st and 2/22nd Battalions are to relive.
the 2/23rd and 2/24th.

The 2/22nd 2/23rd and 2/24th Battalions throughout the scheme are <u>imaginary.</u>

Copy No.

181st INFANTRY BRIGADE. ORDER 118

Spring's Farm
12/1/16.

O.S. ½" No 30.

1. The 2/21st Battalion the London Regiment will relieve the 2/23rd Batt. London Regiment in the trenches and occupy the right sector of the Brigade Frontage from N of ROMAN to south-west of R in Roman Road inclusive. The Battalion will relieve via FEERING TRENCH. The head of the Battn will enter FEERING TRENCH at 5-30 pm.

Imaginary 2. O.C./2/21st Battalion the London Regiment will arrange for the Company Commanders and O.C. M.G. to inspect their portions of the position by daylight.

Imaginary 3. O.C. 2/23rd Battalion the London Regiment will detail the necessary guides, who will meet their reliefs at L of LANGLEY GREEN.

Imaginary 4. Teas will be taken before moving off from billets. COOKERS will not be used. Arrangements must be made for troops to cook breakfast and dinners by means of braziers. The Battalions being relieved will hand over all available braziers, coke and charcoal can be drawn from the refilling point.

Imaginary. 5 Bombs, sandbags, wire, picketing pegs etc from R.E. DEPOT, SKYE GREEN.

6. O.C.2/21st Battalion,London Regt., will report immediately relief is completed.

Imaginary 7. The 2/23rd Batt. London Regt., will take over the 2/21st Batt London Regt billets and report when they have arrived there.

8. Reports to HOWCHINS FARM.

(Signed) J.N.Horlick,
Captain,
Brigade Major,
181st Infantry Brigade.

Issued at   am

Copy No 1 filed
 "   2 Division(telephoned)
 "   3 2/21st Battalion,(telephoned)
 "   4 2/22nd   "   "
 "   5 2/23rd   "   "
 "   6 2/24th   "   "
 "   7 2/6th London Field Ambuland by Orderly
 "   8 A.D.M.S.
 "   9 181st Brigade Coy A.S.C. by Orderly
 " 10 No 3 Section Signal Company.

A map of the Brigade frontage Scale 6" approximately is attached for reference. No information likely to be of use to the enemy is to be written on this map e.g. M.G. positions, Battalion Headquarters etc.

———————

G/ASC.

INSTRUCTIONS.

For the purposes of the scheme the road running from LANGLEY GREEN (called GREEN trench and FEERING trench) will represent communication trenches.

The railway line (MARKS TEY - WITHAM) will represent the support trench.

The MARKS TEY-WITHAM Road will represent the fire trench.

All roads connecting the firing line and support line will represent communication trenches.

All roads running south-east from the fire trench will represent saps.

The enemy's trenches are 100-400 yards distant.

The Brigade has held this portion of the line for 6 days during which time the 2/21st Battalion has been in billets at Coggeshall.

Brigade Headquarters - Howchins Farm.

2/21st Battalion
Regimental Aidpost   - LANGLEY GREEN.

2/21st Batt. Transport- COGGESHALL.

Refilling point   - MARYGOLDS.

BATTALION ORDERS NO 1.

BY MAJOR. B. FLETCHER COMMANDING 2/21st BATTALION, LONDON REGIMENT.

Ref.Map.O.S.½"No 30.   COGGESHALL,
                                                                  19/1/16.

1.   The Battalion will march, order as per margin, to relieve
A.Co less 1   the 2/23rd Battalion, the London Regiment occupying the
Platoon   right sector of trenches from N. of Roman to communication
1 Pltn.A.Co   trench south west (S.W.) of the first R. in ROMAN ROAD .
1.pltnB.Co
C.Co.

                  The Battalion will relieve via FEERING trench.
                  The head of the Battalion will enter FEERING trench at 5.30 pm
                  D.Coy will march direct to billets at Skye Green.
2.
                  Company Commanders, Signalling Officer, and M.G.Officer will
                  be at first L of LANGLEY GREEN at 12 noon to-day.

3.   The distribution will be as per margin.
    Fire trench
A.Co (less 1 plth) From N to M of ROMAN.
B.Co (less 1 pltn) From M of ROMAN to FEERING trench.

    Support trench
1 platoon A.Co
1 platoon B.Co.
    Third Line
C.Coy
    Reserve Coy

D.Coy at SKYE GREEN

4.   Guides will meet the reliefs at L of Langley Green at 5.30
                  pm

5.   O.C. Companies will report immediately they are in position.

6.   Reports to Skye Green.

                                                Capt and Adjutant,
                                                   2/21st Battalion,
                                              The London Regiment .

Issued at 9am
Copy No 1 retained.
  " No 2 181st Infy.Brigade.
  " No 3 A.Coy
  "   " 4 B.Coy
  "   " 5 C.Coy
  "   " 6 D.Coy
  "   " 7 Machine Gun Officer
  "   " 8 Signalling Officer.
  "   " 9 Medical Officer.

Copy   NOTES ON RELIEVING etc. IN TRENCHES.

Two Battalions of a Brigade are in the front line.
Two Battalions of a Brigade are in reserve in billets.
The same Battalions always relieve one another.
Battalions do six days in and six days back.

Two Companies in the firing line for 48 hours on end as a rule
One platoon from each of the above companies in support.
Two Companies back behind in either dug outs or billets.
In reserve. They do all fatigues, carrying etc.
(For purposes of scheme have 2 Companies in Fire Trench and
2 in support)

Ammunition

200 rounds on the men.
100 rounds per man in the trenches in boxes.
All these boxes come from the Brigade Reserve. All Battalion
ammunition carts are always to be kept perfectly full.

All communication trenches should be either numbered or marked
with a name, also latrines, ammunition stores, Bombs, Signal Posts
etc.

Reliefs going up Communication trenches, must move very slowly
indeed(1 mile - 1¼ miles an hour) Touch must never be lost.
Platoons move close up to each other.
Each Company has a guide.
On arrival in trenches Bayonets are immediately fixed.
Every sentry to have a periscope. In fire trench at nights
men sleep on each side of look out man 1 in 3 on lookout)

Men always to be thickest where Units join at Saps etc.

Machine Guns should always command saps etc with enfilade or
raking fire. Only single shots to be fired from Battle position.

ENEMY TRENCH 2/21st.

No 1 Sap

No 2 Sap

FIRE TRENCH

2/21st.
Support Trench

FEERING TRENCH

GREEN TRENCH

6" = 1 mile

REPORT ON TACTICAL SCHEME AT FEERING

ON 19th JANUARY 1916.

BY

CAPT. AND ADJUTANT A.J.WALTER.

++++++++++++++++

The exercise was somewhat hampered by bad weather. The relief was conducted via FEERING TRENCH. The leading Company failed to realise the fact that roads represented trenches, and consequently the rate was considerably faster than that possible in trenches. This caused gaps in the line which were hard to rectify and rendered communication and guidance difficult.

On arrival at the front line and support trenches some confusion was caused by one company not filling the firing bays as they arrived-going instead to the farthest limitb of their front and filling this bay first. Had this been actually in a trench considerable confusion and delay would have been caused. This was pointed out.

Bayonets were fixed and sentries posted, also all sanitary and other arrangements made promptly.

Communications   Communication between front firing line and HEADQUARTERS by telephone was opened in 10 minutes and maintained with brief interruption (owing to breakages etc)throughout.

Medical   Regimental Aid Posts were established with a main dressing station at LANGLEY GREEN.

Ammunition etc   Satisfactory arrangements were made for passing up ammunition, food etc.

The Exercise closed at 12.30 pm

A.J.Walter
Capt & Adj

20th January '16

Confidential

Vol. 2 No. 2

War Diary
of the
2/21st Battalion London Regiment
from
1st to 29th February 1916.

Army Form C. 2118.

WAR DIARY
or
INTELLIGENCE SUMMARY.
(Erase heading not required.)

Ref:- Ord Survey Sheet 282 1" = 1 mile

Instructions regarding War Diaries and Intelligence Summaries are contained in F. S. Regs., Part II. and the Staff Manual respectively. Title pages will be prepared in manuscript.

Place	Date	Hour	Summary of Events and Information	Remarks and references to Appendices
	1916			
SUTTON VENY	1st Feb	7.30 am	Parade by Platoons.	See Appendix I
		9 am	Parade by Companies } Instruction in accordance 60th (LONDON) DIVISIONAL Letter dated 27th January 1916. Based on War Office letter 9/General No./5757 (M.T.2) dated 23/12/15.	
		2 pm	Parade by Companies	Appx.
			Weather - Fine	
"	2nd Feb	7.30 am	Parade by Platoons for squad drill	
		9 am	Company parades, squad & company drill, musketry, physical training	
		2 pm	Orders received expressing FIELD MARSHALL E LORD FRENCH'S satisfaction at inspection on 31st January 1916. Weather - Fine.	See Appx II
"	3rd Feb	7.30 am	Parade by Platoons for squad drill	
		9 am	Lectures & instruction on musketry in huts. Physical drill in huts	
		2 pm	Lectures and instruction in huts.	
			Weather - Very wet making outdoor instruction impossible.	Appx
"	4th Feb	7.30 am	Instruction in huts. - Musketry. Physical exercise etc	
		-4pm	Weather - Rainy. Condition of ground makes outdoor instruction difficult	Appx
"	5th Feb	7.30 am	Squad drill under platoon commanders	Appx
		9 am	Physical training	

WAR DIARY
or
INTELLIGENCE SUMMARY.
(Erase heading not required.)

Army Form C. 2118.

Instructions regarding War Diaries and Intelligence Summaries are contained in F.S. Regs., Part II. and the Staff Manual respectively. Title pages will be prepared in manuscript.

Place	Date	Hour	Summary of Events and Information	Remarks and references to Appendices
SUTTON VENY	1916			
	6th Feb	10.15 am	Interior economy. Weather:- Fine	
"	6th Feb	9 am	Church Parade. Weather:- Fine	Apps.
"	7th Feb	7.30 am	Squad drill with arms	Apps.
		9.30 am	Route march. Route taken:- BOREHAM - HEYTESBURY - TYTHERINGTON - SUTTON VENY. Distance :- 7 miles. No casualties. Weather:- Rainy	Apps.
"	8th Feb	7.30 am	Squad drill with arms.	
		9.30 - 4 pm	Training motor company arrangements in accordance with War Office letter 91/Spyvad No/5757 (MT2) dated 23/1/16. Weather:- Fine	See Appen. I
"	9th Feb	7.30 am	Squad drill with arms	Apps.
		9.30 - 4 pm	Training motor company arrangements as on the 8th Feb 1916. Weather:- Cold + Fine	Apps.
"	10th Feb	7.30 am	Squad drill with arms	
		9 am - 4 pm 6 pm	Training motor company arrangements as on the 8th Feb 1916. 2/LIEUTS E.L. SPENCER and R.H. ALDIS report for duty from WINCHESTER (Authority LONDON DISTRICT ORDER No 19 para 6 of 22-1-16)	Apps.

Army Form C. 2118.

WAR DIARY
or
INTELLIGENCE SUMMARY.

(Erase heading not required.)

Instructions regarding War Diaries and Intelligence Summaries are contained in F. S. Regs., Part II. and the Staff Manual respectively. Title pages will be prepared in manuscript.

Place	Date	Hour	Summary of Events and Information	Remarks and references to Appendices
SUTTON VENY	1916 10th Dec		Weather - Fine	gjs
"	11th "	7.30	Parade under Platoon Commanders for squad drill etc	
		9am - 4pm	Parade in accordance with War Office letter 9/General No/5757 (MT 2) dated 27/9/15.	gjs
			Weather. Fine generally but with occasional rain.	
	12th	7.30 am	Parade under Platoon Commanders for squad drill etc	
		9am	Company parade for musketry etc	
		2pm	Company parade for physical exercises	
			Weather :- Fine	gjs
	13th	10.20 am	Church Parade.	
		11 am	60th (LONDON) DIVISIONAL ORDER increasing local leave to 10% received	gjs
			Weather :- Rainy.	
	14th	7.30 am	Parade under Platoon Commanders for squad drill etc	
		6.45	"D" Company commenced musketry course.	gjs
	15th	9am	Company Parade for musketry etc.	
		7.30 am	Parade under Platoon Commanders for squad drill etc.	
		8.45	C. Company commenced musketry course.	gjs

Army Form C. 2118.

WAR DIARY
or
INTELLIGENCE SUMMARY.
(Erase heading not required.)

Instructions regarding War Diaries and Intelligence Summaries are contained in F. S. Regs., Part II. and the Staff Manual respectively. Title pages will be prepared in manuscript.

Place	Date	Hour	Summary of Events and Information	Remarks and references to Appendices
SUTTON VENY	1916			
	15th Feb		Weather :- Rain ceased	OPS
	16th Feb	9.15 am	Battalion Parade for Divisional Exercise	
		1.30 pm	Divisional exercise cancelled owing to weather conditions	
		9 am	"B" Coy firing miniature range course	
		2 pm	A C + D Coys musketry in huts	
			Weather :- Rain ceased	
	17th Feb	9.15 am	Battalion Parade for Divisional Exercise	OPS
		9 am	Weather :- Fine	
	18th Feb	7.30 am	Parade cancelled owing to rain	OPS
		9 am	A Coy. Commence miniature range course	
			B.C+D. Physical drill musketry in huts	
		11 am.	Inspection of transport by MAJOR LANDON C.B. INSPECTOR GENERAL OF Q.M.G. SERVICES	See Appendix III
		2 pm	Musketry in huts. Weather :- Rain	
	19th Feb	7.30 am	Squad drill with arms.	OPS
		9 am	Physical training musketry	See Appendix IV

Army Form C. 2118.

WAR DIARY
or
INTELLIGENCE SUMMARY.
(Erase heading not required.)

Instructions regarding War Diaries and Intelligence Summaries are contained in F. S. Regs., Part II. and the Staff Manual respectively. Title pages will be prepared in manuscript.

Place	Date	Hour	Summary of Events and Information	Remarks and references to Appendices
	1916			
SUTTON VENY	19th Feb	11.30 a.m.	Division economy fire drill. Weather - fine generally but with some rain	GpS
	20th Feb	8.45 a.m.	Church Parade. Weather - fine	GpS
	21st Feb	9 a.m.	Musketry on open range cancelled owing to rain storms	
		9 a.m.	Musketry, physical drill etc in huts.	
			CAPT A.G. MACDONALD takes over duties of Adjutant since CAPT A.J. WALTER who vacates	Opt.
			(Authority:- LONDON GAZETTE. dated 21-2-1916) Weather - Rain showers	
	22nd Feb	3.15pm	Inspection of horses by LIEUT-COL H.M. FERRAR, INSPECTOR OF REMOUNTS.	See Appendix V
		8 a.m.	385 Officers NCO's & men fired Practices 1º, 2º Short Musketry Course. Weather fine	GpS
		9 a.m.	Remainder of Battalion - Musketry, Bayonet fighting & Physical Training	
		2 pm	Remainder of Battalion - Extended Order Drill	
		3 - 4 pm	94 men vaccinated 60th =(LONDON) DIVISIONAL LETTER A/333/32 received increasing Xmas hours to 10%.	GM.
	23rd Feb	7.30	Squad drill	
		9 a.m.	Musketry - Physical Training - Bayonet fighting	
		11 a.m.	Inspection of lamps by A.Q.M.G SOUTHERN COMMAND	
		2 pm	Company Training on Area A3. Weather - fine very cold	GM.
	24th Feb	8 a.m.	Route march cancelled owing to weather. Weather - Snow Storms	

1577 Wt.W10791/1773 500,000 1/15 D. D. & L. A.D.S.S./Forms/C. 2118.

Army Form C. 2118.

WAR DIARY
or
INTELLIGENCE SUMMARY.
(Erase heading not required.)

Instructions regarding War Diaries and Intelligence Summaries are contained in F. S. Regs., Part II. and the Staff Manual respectively. Title pages will be prepared in manuscript.

Place	Date	Hour	Summary of Events and Information	Remarks and references to Appendices
SUTTON VENY	1916			
	Feb 24th	9.30am & 2pm	Musketry, Physical Training etc in Barrack Rooms + Huts. 218 NCOs & men vaccinated	Jm.
"	Feb 25th	8 am	Weather – Heavy Snowfall	
		9 am	Training in Barrack Rooms – Musketry & Physical Training	
		2 pm	Companies marched to Area A 3 – returned at 3.30 on account of bad weather. Second Lieutenants C.E. REYNOLDS, F.D. LEVY, F.G. BARRETT, R.W. BRETT to be temporary lieutenants dated 1/1/16 (Authority LONDON GAZETTE 18th February 1916) CAPTAIN A.J. WALTER takes over command of 'D' Coy	Jm.
"	Feb 26th	7.30 am	Cleaning equipment & arms	
		9.0		
		11.0 am	Kit Dress	
		11.30	Interior Economy by all Companies	Jm.
		2.30 pm	Battalion Games	Jm.
"	Feb 27th	11.15 am	Church Parade	
"	Feb 28th	7.30 am	Squad Drill	
		9-12 noon	Musketry – Bayonet Fighting + Physical Training	Thaw – some snow fell. Thaw set in.

Army Form C. 2118.

WAR DIARY
or
INTELLIGENCE SUMMARY.
(Erase heading not required.)

Instructions regarding War Diaries and Intelligence Summaries are contained in F. S. Regs., Part II. and the Staff Manual respectively. Title pages will be prepared in manuscript.

Place	Date	Hour	Summary of Events and Information	Remarks and references to Appendices
	1916			
SUTTON VENY	Feb 26th	2 pm	Company Training on Area A 3 Weather fine	
		2 pm	60 NCO's own first Practice No 62? Snipers Musketry Course on D Range	Lyn
	Feb 28th		Bivouacs Scheme of Trench digging commenced Weather fine	
		8.30 am	Trench digging party 120 men of "A" Coy	
		9.30 am	Musketry – Physical Drill – Bayonet fighting by Companies	
		1.30 pm	Trench digging party 140 men of "B" Coy	
		2 pm	Musketry Training	
		4.15 pm	Staff Officer for Brentons inspected Army Book 164 at Orderly Room	Lyn

SUTTON VENY
2.3.16

J Fletcher Lieut-Col
O.C. 2/21st Battn LONDON REGT

Copy   Appendix I

With reference to the Syllabus of Training issued with War Office Letter 9/General No./5757 (M.T.2) dated 23rd December, 1915, the General Officer Commanding directs that the following training be carried out during the first week, commencing 1st February:-

7.30am Parade by Platoons (without arms) Platoons to double short distance up to 200 yards at a steady double, attention being paid that the sections of fours keep closed up.   Ten minutes is then to be spent in practising forming fours and turnings. Then a steady double of 200 yards followed by ten minutes of moving in fours and forming to right and left in quick time. The parade to finish by all platoons doubling off to private parades where they will dismiss.

8am. Breakfasts.

9am Parade by Companies. All men to be cleaned and shaved.

9.30am Squad drill without arms, turnings, forming of fours, and formations in fours.(Infantry Training Sects 10 to 46)

9.30am Physical Training. to 10.30 am

11am   **Trained Soldiers**
to   Lectures on Musketry by Company Commanders.
12 noon   Practising men to bring up their rifles correctly and quickly to the shoulder in all firing positions.

        Recruits
        Lectures on Musketry. Aiming Instruction. Firing Positions.(Musketry Regs Part 1, Chapter IV).

2pm-3pm Parade under Platoon Commanders. Squad Drill fours forming to right and left, forming columns of sections and files, marking time, side step, stopping short.
3pm-3.10pm Platoons double for 200 yards in fours, and then double to private parades where they will dismiss.
3.15-3.30pm Lecture on Care of Arms by Platoon Commanders.
3.30pm to 3.45 pm Saluting.

               SECOND WEEK.
Same as first week, except that all squad drills by the trained men will be in drill order with arms; fixing and unfixing bayonets. Recruits will follow the detail laid down in the Syllabus.

Doubling to be increased to 300 yards and route marches to be for seven miles.

                      (sgnd)E.T.Humphreys,
                            Lt-Col,
                           General Staff,
Sutton Veny,   60th(London) Division.
  27th January 1916.

COPY

NOTES

1. Steady doubling must be insisted on, and fours must be so closed up that, if halted and turned to right or left, no intervals exist.

2. All young Officers and N.C.Os must learn the details of squad and platoon drill. Words of command must be given correctly and in such a manner that they can be acted on smartly.

3. Route Marching is to be carried out once a week by each Battalion. Total distance to be marched to be about six miles. Dress to be marching order. First line Transport to be taken. Further details as to roads and days available for Units will be issued.

4. All the parades except route marching will be carried out in drill order. Rifles will be carried only during route marches and on the parade between 11 a.m. and 12 noon, when the firing positions are being practised.

5. On wet days when it is not advisable to take the men out, the following training can be carried out in the huts :-
   (a) Physical Training.
   (b) Lectures on Musketry, Rapid Loading, Firing Positions.
   (c) Fitting of marching order.
   (d) Teaching men how to get up quickly from the Prone Position when dressed in Marching Order.

6. It is recognised that, owing to difficulties as regards Parade Grounds, e.g. Size of Battalion Parade Ground and distance of other suitable ground from huts, the above programme cannot be rigidly adhered to, especially as regards times. The G.O.C. however wishes Units to be trained as far as possible on the lines given so that the spirit of the W.O. letter may be carried out. If the Battalion Parade Ground is not large enough to be used by the whole Battalion, it should be reserved for the recruits when they are being trained separately and the trained men should be exercised on some field or open ground away from the Battalion huts.

7. Recruits and Trained soldiers will be exercised together in the training ordered at 7-30 a.m. from 3 to 3-45 p.m. and during route marches.

(Sgd) G.T.HUMPHREYS Lt. Col.

G.S. 60th Div.

APPENDIX II

EXTRACT FROM 60th (LONDON) DIVISION (T.F.) ORDERS BY MAJOR GENERAL
E.S.BULFIN, C.V.O., C.B. COMMANDING.

1st February, 1916.

The G.O.C. has pleasure in intimating to all Ranks in the Division, that Field-Marshall Lord French, on the occasion of his inspection yesterday (31st January, 1916), expressed his satisfaction with the turn-out of the Troops of the 60th (London) Division and with their bearing under arms.

He considers the steadiness of the men under arms, and the method of handling their arms, reflects credit on all Ranks, and he directs that this expression of opinion be conveyed to all concerned.

Ref. ORDNANCE SURVEY SHEET 122
      1" = 1 Mile   APPENDIX III

60TH (LONDON) DIVISION
=====oOo=====

TACTICAL EXERCISE HELD ON 17TH FEBUARY 1916

Division deploying for attack

A frontal attack combined with a flank attack.

CONTENTS

1. Situation
2. Divisional Orders
3. Brigade Orders
4. Précis of remarks by G.O.C. 60th (LONDON) DIVISION.

DIVISIONAL EXERCISE - 16th FEBRUARY, 1916.

1. The Division deploying for attack.
2. A frontal attack combined with a flank attack.

SITUATION.

Ref: 1" O.S. 32, and
1" O.S. 122.

A raiding force, of which the 3rd Corps (comprising the 60th and 61st Divisions) forms a part, has landed on the South Coast and is moving Northwards. The enemy is hastily sending troops Southwards to meet the invaders.

The 3rd Corps has been pushed on in advance to seize the junction at WESTBURY, and on the night of the 15th-16th has reached the L.& S.W.R: the 60th Division about SEMLEY and the 61st Division about GILLINGHAM.

At 6 a.m. 16th February, the G.O.C., 60th Division receives the following message :-

detraining at WARMINSTER.

"Sixtieth Division.   G 42   Sixteenth.
"Enemy reliably reported to be holding high ground East
"and West of BRIXTON DEVERILL with a weak Division AAA
"Hostile reinforcements are expected to reach that position
"by 1 p.m. today AAA Sixtieth Division will attack enemy
"between Point 745 PARSONAGE DOWN - where his left flank is
"believed to rest - and Point 784 LITTLE DOWN (exclusive) AAA
"Sixty-first Division will attack from Point 784 (inclusive)
"to COLD KITCHEN HILL AAA Attacks to commence at 11 a.m., at
"which hour leading attacking troops should cross the line
"CHICKLADE - KILMINGTON AAA Every endeavour is to be made
"to drive the enemy Westwards AAA Corps orders follow AAA
"Acknowledge
            Third Corps - 5 a.m."

On receipt of this message, the G.O.C., Sixtieth Division, issues orders for the move to the places of assembly prior to the attack on the enemy.

Copies to :-
Infantry Brigade Headquarters	9
Infantry Battalions	60
R.A. Headquarters	3
Brigades and Batteries	12
C.R.E. and Field Companies	6
Divisional Headquarters	10
	100

60 th London Divisional Order No: 10

16th Feb. 1916

Information
(1) Enemy is reported to be holding the high ground East and West of BRIXTON DEVERAL with a weak Division, in order to cover the detrainment at WARMINSTER of reinforcements which are due at that station at noon today. The 3rd Corps is to attack this Division and drive it Westwards. The 60th Division attacks on the right and the 61st Division on the left. The Corps Artillery will bombard the enemy's position for an hour prior to the Infantry attack commencing, paying particular attention to BEECH CLUMP. It will also establish a barrage of fire from 11 a.m. to 2 p.m. on the roads and tracks leading south from LONGBRIDGE DEVERAL and TYTHERINGTON.

Intention
(2) The 60th Division will attack from Point 745 to BEECH CLUMP exclusive as under. The attack to commence at 11 a.m. The object of the attack is to drive in the enemy's left flank.
    (a) 181st Infantry Bde (less one Battalion, Divn Res.) and 3/3rd Field Coy. R.E. will attack Point 745 to the EAST KNOYLE-LONGBRIDGE DEVERAL Road (inclusive to BEECH CLUMP (exclusive)
    (b) The 180th Infantry Brigade (less and 1/6th Field Company R.E. will attack from the LONGBRIDGE DEVERAL road (exclusive) to BEECH CLUMP (exclusive

Time
(3) The left attack will commence at 11 a.m. The right attack will be echeloned in rear of the left attack at a distance of about 800 yards, moving forward at 11.10 a.m.

Artillery
(4) The 2/5th F.A.B. will support the right attack and the 2/7th F.A.B. the left attack.
    The 2/21st Battery will support both attacks.
    All the Artillery will open fire at 10.30 a.m.

Divisional Reserve
(5) The 179th Infy Bde and 2/4th Field Coy R.E. will be in Divisional Reserve and will follow in rear of the right attack and on its outer flank. One Battalion 181st Brigade will remain at the Assembly place.

Consolidation
(6) As soon as the position has been gained, it is to be consolidated under arrangements to be made by the Officers Commanding 180th and 181st Infy, Bdes about 6 stripes of trench each 100 yds in length being dug by these Brigades. The Field Coys allotted to these brigades are to have special tactical points allotted to them for consolidation. The further driving back of the enemy will be the task of the Divisional Reserve or other available troops under Divisional arrangements. When the forward position has been captured, each Artillery Brigade will send forward a Battery to give close support to the Infantry Brigade which it is supporting.

Cyclists
(7) a. The Cyclist Coy (less one platoon) will detail patrols to find out any advanced positions held by the enemy and also the position of his left flank. SHERRINGTON and CORTON are to be kept under constant observation and reports sent back every half hour as to any enemy movements in that direction.
    b. One platoon Cyclist Coy. is to keep touch with the 61st Division. Reports are to be sent back every half hour as to the progress being made by the 61st Division.

Reports
(8) Reports to farm ½ mile W. of KNOYLE DOWN FARM, after 10.30 a.m.,

E.T.HUMPHREYS Lt. Col.
GENERAL STAFF

Issued at 9.30 a.m. to
Div,H.Q.	3		
C.R.A.	4	180th Bde	1
C.R.E.	1	181st Bde	1
A.D.M.S.	1	Cyclist Coy	1
179th Bde,	1		

181st BRIGADE ORDER NO: 1

Ref. O.S. 1"
SHEET 122

SUTTON VENY
No: 2 CAMP
15-2-16

1. The Brigade will take part in the Divisional Operations tomorrow 16-2-16, and will march out to the Place of Assembly (TWO MILE DOWN). The Head of the column passing the starting point THE SOUTH WEST ENTRANCE to the BRIGADE CAMP at 7.05 a.m.

2. Order of march as shewn in margin

24th Batt
23rd Batt
22nd Batt
21st Batt

3. Route SUTTON VENY - LONGBRIDGE DEVERILL - EAST KNOYLE

4. 1st Line Transport as laid down in Divisional Instructions will accompany units.

(sd) J.C.Horlick
Capt,
Brigade Major
181st Infantry Brigade,

Issued at 9 a.m. to

    Divi H.Q.   1 COPY
    2/21st Batt   1 Copy
    2/22nd Batt   1 Copy
    2/23rd Batt   1 Copy
    2/24th Batt   1 Copy

Officer Commanding
    181st Infantry Brigade
        The Tactical Exercise postponed to-day will be carried out tomorrow.
        All arrangements will be made as for to-day.
        (sd) C.A.Bolton
                      Capt.
                  GENERAL STAFF
SUTTON VENY   60th (LONDON) Division
16-2-16

Officer Commanding
    2/21st Battn. London Regt.
        The above is forwarded for your information and action
                    J.N. Horlick
No 2 Camp   Capt
SUTTON VENY   Brigade Major
16/2/16   181st Infantry Brigade

Appendix III

2/21st BATTALION, THE LONDON REGIMENT.

PROGRAMME OF TRAINING FOR WEEK COMMENCING 17/4/16

MONDAY 17/4/16	7-0 – 7-45 a.m.	Drill Parade.	9-30 a.m. 9-30 a.m.	Route March "C" Co. 12 Officers and N.C.Os Wire Entanglement Instruction.
			2-0 p.m.	"A" Co. Obstacle Course. General Training under Co. arrangements.
TUESDAY 18/4/16	7-0 – 7-45 a.m.	Drill Parade.	9-30 a.m.	Company Training on Area Nr. North Farm. "A" Co. 12 Officers and N.C.Os Wire Entanglement Instruction.
			2-0 p.m. 8-0 p.m.	General Training under Company arrangements. 50 men from each "A", "C" & "D" Cos. Night Digging.
WEDNESDAY 19/4/16.			8-45 a.m. 11-15 a.m.	Battalion Digging. 196 men of "A", "B" & "D" Companies. Semaphore Drill. "D" Co. 12 Officers and N.C.Os Wire Entanglement Instruction.
			2-0 p.m.	Company Training in Camp "D" Co. Obstacle Course.
THURSDAY 20/4/16.	7-0 – 7-45 a.m.	Drill Parade.	9-30 a.m.	Company Training on Cotley Hill. "B" Co. 12 Officers and N.C.Os Wire Entanglement Instruction.
			2-0 p.m.	General Training under Company arrangements. 50 men from each "A", "B" & "D" Companies. Night Digging.
FRIDAY 21/4/16				G O O D F R I D A Y.
SATURDAY 22/4/16.	7-0 – 7-45 a.m.	Drill Parade.	9-0 a.m.	Parade under Coy. arrangements – Interior Economy, Fire Drill etc.
SUNDAY 23/4/16				C H U R C H P A R A D E

Officer Commanding

    181st Infantry Brigade

1-   Each Infantry Brigade on the march out to the rendez-vous will drop a company to act as covering troops to the Division during assembly preparatory to attack.

2.   The line to be held by these outposts will be :-

STONEHILL COPSE (WESTERN END OF GREAT RIDGE WOOD) - PERTWOOD
    LOWER PERTWOOD FARM.

3.   This line will be occupied as follows:-

179th Infantry Brigade (1 Company)
    STONEHILL COPSE - CRATT HILL (junction of paths $\frac{1}{4}$ mile North
        of point 739 (inclusive)

181st Infantry Brigade (1 Company)
    CRATT HILL (junction of paths $\frac{1}{4}$ mile N. of point 739 (exclusive)
        to EAST KNOYLE - LONGBRIDGE DEVERILL ROAD (exclusive)

180th Infantry Brigade (1 Company)
    EAST KNOYLE - LONGBRIDGE DEVERILL ROAD (inclusive) Pt 739 555
        on HINDON - MONKTON DEVERILL ROAD.

The Divisional Cyclist Company will furnish a picquet on the extreme right flank on TUMULUS $\frac{3}{4}$ Mile N of ROWDEAN HILL

4.   Each Infantry Brigade will furnish 1 N.C.O. and 2 men as Signallers for Divisional Headquarters to report at the point of assembly at Pt 654 at 10.30 a.m. to-morrow.

                      (sd) C.A.BOLTON Capt.
                            General Staff
Sutton Veny   60th (LONDON) Division.
15-2-16

Officer Commanding

    2/21st Battn.

        The above is forwarded for your information.

                            J.N.HORLICK
                                Capt.
                          Brigade Major
SUTTON VENY   181st Infantry Brigade
15-2-16

PRÉCIS of REMARKS BY G.O.C. 60th (LONDON) DIVISION
by Capt and Adj. A.J.Walter.
=================

ORDERS   It is impossible to state that a certain thing such as a "Counter Attack" <u>will</u> take place at a certain fixed time. Officers must be prepared to launch attacks, etc., or to act at the crucial moment.

GENERAL FAULTS   Q 1.   <u>Lack of co-operation and communication</u>   This was very noticable and the attack was frittered away by small local attacks and would probably have failed. The lack of efficient communication was probably caused by the number of signallers away on courses of instruction.

FAULTS IN ATTACK.   Artillery formation was retained too long. Units in the majority of cases can over the skyline in artillery formation at a distance of under 2000 yards. This would have entailed very heavy losses.

     Loss of direction owing to obstacles crossing the path diagonally was also very noticable. Firing positions were occupied diagonal to and even at right angles to the enemy's position.

     When in artillery formation the small columns were very often halted near to trees bushes or other similar easy ranging marks.

     On several occasions lines were halted on the forward slopes of hills and the men consequently offered better targets.

     Advancing infantry on one occasion passed right through a battery occupying a forward position rendering this battery useless.

     Fire was commenced at long ranges and died down and in some cases ceased altogether at the shorter ranges. Firing ceased altogether while the men fixed bayonets.

     Brigades in both instances did not conform to the frontage allotted to them. In one case 500 yards was reduced to 300 and in another case 600 yards was increased to 1500 yards.

     Brigade reserves in both instances were too far behind

COPY

Appendix IV

D.S.T.

1st Line Transport, 60th (2/2nd. (London) Division
Sutton Veny, 18-2-16

181st Brigade
2/6th London Field Ambulance.

The weather was very bad during my inspection and I made every allowance for that and the muddy state of the camps.

Units have not yet received the Limbered G.S.Wagons in accordance with Part VII, War Establishments. These wagons are expected very shortly and in the meantime G.S.Mark X Wagons are on charge.

The Field Ambulance require G.S.Wagons to replace those at present on charge which are not of Army pattern - This can be done as soon as the Infantry Bns. of the Division receive the Limbered G.S. due to them.

The travelling kitchens of all units require thorough overhauling, especially as regards the stew pots before they can be considered fit for work overseas. Most of the stew pots are rusty and in the case of some Battalions have been neglected.

Girths of draught mules too far forward, and in one case caused a bad gall at the elbow.

There was in several Battalions evidence of a want of looking round by Transport Officers and Sergts. before marching off, which would have enabled many defects to have been remedied. Rear girths of Pack mules in many cases badly adjusted - A web connecting strap would keep the girths in the right position, but carelessness in not pulling the girths sufficiently tight was apparent in some Battalions.

Nearly every Battalion requires to give more careful attention to the fitting of the breechings on draught animals. It was explained in some cases that changes of horses and mules caused this, but there is no reason why animals should be working with breechings hanging down to the hocks and practically falling off the animals backs. - Even when the breechings were capable of being fitted by simply taking up straps or punching a few holes, this was neglected.

In some Battalions drivers were wearing unnecessarily sharp spurs.

Drivers require considerably more instruction in getting the off animal to move with the near one. Drivers start the animal they are riding and leave the own off animal to its own devices.

There were many deficiencies of drivers short whips.

The transport of the undermentioned Battalions was below the average in efficiency :-

2/22nd Bn. London Regt.- Harness required considerable attention, both as to condition and fitting.
Stew pots of kitchens neglected.
Girths of pack mules under sheaths.
Transport Officer absent sick.

2/23rd Bn. London Rgt.- Want of atten-tion in details in connection with putting on harness which could have been obviated by inspection before leaving quarters.
Transport Officer absent sick.
Pack animals girths badly adjusted.

With the exception of the points I have referred to the 1st Line Transport of the Division generally should soon reach a satisfactory standard of efficiency, especially in the case of the 179th Brigade.

There were several articles of equipment due to units which are receiving careful attention, and which the D.A.D.O.S. assured me would very shortly be provided.

(Sgd) F.W.B.LANDON
Major General
C.I.Q.M.G.S.

19-2-15

COPY   C.R., S.C., No. 90665/25 (R)   Appendix V.

Date of Inspection Feb. 21st 1916.

60th (London) Division.

Unit and Company 181st Infantry Bde.	<u>Units</u> Headquarters 2/21st Battn. 2/22nd " 2/23rd " 2/24th "
Place. Sutton Veny	

Condition. This Brigade looks extremely well.

Class and Numbers H.Q. 9 Riders, 10 Mules   ) Pack
                      2/21st. 14 Cobs. 6 H.D. 32 L.D.   ) H.D.
                      2/23rd. 63 in all. 2/24th 64 in all) Riders
) & L.D.

Feeding. 3 times. I saw some very bad hay but was unable to obtain label.

Bedding. Practically none.

Farrier. Reported satisfactory.

Chaff Cutters. 1 per Brigade.

Corn Crushers. -

Sprays. -

Canadians. quite a number.

Pamphlet. Yes

Horse Management. Very good.

Room for horses. Congested. No. room.

Ringworm. Nil

Mange. Nil

Strangles. Nil

Branding. Satisfactory

Shoeing. Satisfactory

Remarks. The stables of this Brigade are in very bad order, some of the standings in shocking order - notwithstanding the horses look very well indeed and are a credit to the Brigade.

                                           (Sgd)   H.M.FERRAR Lt.-Col.
                                                                 I of R.

Feb. 21st 1916.

Vol 2. No 3.

Confidential

War Diary
of the
2/21st Battalion London Regt.
from
1st to 31st March 1916.

Army Form C. 2118.

WAR DIARY or INTELLIGENCE SUMMARY.
(Erase heading not required)

Instructions regarding War Diaries and Intelligence Summaries are contained in F.S. Regs., Part II. and the Staff Manual respectively. Title pages will be prepared in manuscript.

Ref. O.S. Sheets nos. 122 & 123 1" to 1 mile

Place	Date	Hour	Summary of Events and Information	Remarks and references to Appendices
	1916			
SUTTON VENY	Mar 1	9.30	Battalion Training - Outpost Scheme & Lewis Machine Guns received	Eng.
"	" 2	7.30		
"	" 3	tee	General Training in Camp.	Eng.
"	" 4	4.5pm		
"	" 5	9am	Church Parade	Eng.
"	6/11		Training as per weekly Programme	Eng.
"		6.15	400 S.M.L.E rifles received 700 Bayonets received	Appens. 1
	Mar 12		Church Parade	
"	" 13/18		Training as per weekly Programme	Eng. Appendix III
"	" 15		Draft of 42 arrived from 104 PROV. BATTALION	
"	" "		26 men of draft from PROV. BATTALION sent to 2/17th & 2/18th BATT. LONDON REGIMENT &c	Eng.
"	" 19	11.15	Draft from 104th PROV. BATTALION inspected by G.O.C. at Headquarters	Eng.
"	" 20/27		Battalion on Brigade + Divisional Duties	Eng. Appens III
"	28/31		General Musketry Course commenced "D" Coy firing General Training as per weekly Programme.	Eng. Appens IV

Greaves Capt Adjt
2/21st Batt Lon. Reg.

Appendix 1

2/21st BATTALION, THE LONDON REGIMENT.

TRAINED MEN'S PROGRAMME OF TRAINING FOR WEEK COMMENCING 6th MARCH 1916.

MONDAY 6/3/16	7-30 – 8-0 a.m. Drill & Doubling.	9-30 a.m. Battalion Route March and practice Night Outposts.
TUESDAY 7/3/16.	7-30 – 8-0 a.m. Drill & Doubling.	9-30 a.m. "A" & "B" Cos. Digging. "C" & "D" Cos. Drill, Physical Training & Bayonet 2-0 p.m. "C" & "D" Cos. Digging. "A" & "B" Cos. ditto. (Fighting).
WEDNESDAY 8/3/16.	7-30 – 8-0 a.m. Drill & Doubling.	9-30 a.m. & Drill, Bayonet Fighting & Physical 6-0 – 9-0 p.m. Night Outposts 2-0 p.m. Training by Company and Platoon Commanders.
THURSDAY 9/3/16½	7-30 – 8-0 a.m. Drill & Doubling.	9-30 a.m. Battalion Training on Area A. 4-30 p.m. Foot Inspection.
FRIDAY 10/3/16.	7-30 – 8-0 a.m. Drill & Doubling.	9-0 a.m. – Company Training on Area A.2. 2-0 – 4-15 p.m. Drill. 4-30 p.m. Pay 12-30 p.m. (Middle Hill). Parade.
SATURDAY 11/3/16.	7-30 – 8-0 a.m. Drill & Doubling.	9-30 – 11 a.m. Physical Training, Bayonet Fighting, Fire Drill. 11-15 a.m. – Interior 9-0 a.m. Remaining men fire Practices 1 & 2a. 12-30 p.m. Economy by Companies.
SUNDAY 12/3/16		C H U R C H P A R A D E

If weather on any of the above days is unfavourable for outdoor work :-
7-30 – 8-0 a.m.   9-30 a.m. – 12-30 p.m.   2-0 – 5-0 p.m.
Hut Inspection.   Physical Training, Musketry, particularly positions   Bayonet Fighting, Musketry,
Rapid Loading, Rapid Aiming & Rapid Firing.   & Lectures.
Lectures.

SUTTON VENY.
4th March 1916.

CAPT. & ADJUTANT.
2/21st Battalion,
THE LONDON REGIMENT.

Appendix II

2/21st BATTALION, THE LONDON REGIMENT

TRAINED MEN'S PROGRAMME OF TRAINING FOR WEEK COMMENCING 13/3/16

MONDAY 13/3/16.
7-30 - 8-0 a.m. Squad Drill Doubling 400 yds.
9-30 a.m. Battalion Training on Cotley Hill (Level ground on the summit)
1-45 p.m. 150 men fire Practices 1a & 2a on Range "D".

TUESDAY 14/3/16.
7-30 - 8-0 a.m. Squad Drill Doubling 400 yds.
9-30 a.m. Battalion Route March and Outpost Scheme.

WEDNESDAY 15/3/16.
7-30 - 8-0 a.m. Squad Drill. Doubling 400 yds.
9-0 a.m. 80 men of "A" Co. & 80 men of "B" Co. Digging.
9-30 a.m. "C" & "D" Co. Company Training on Cotley Hill Artillery Formations - Extended Order Drill - Visual Training - Judging Distance.
2-0 p.m. Physical Training.
3-0 p.m. Musketry. (Rapid Loading Test)

THURSDAY 16/3/16.
7-30 a.m. Emergency Alarm Practice.
9-0 a.m. Firing Party to "D" Range.
9-30 a.m. Remainder of Battalion - Coy. Training etc. (as on Wednesday) on Cotley Hill.
1-30 p.m. "C" Company - Digging.
2-0 p.m. Physical Training - Bayonet Fighting - Musketry (Rapid Aiming Test).
4-30 p.m. Foot Inspth.

FRIDAY 17/3/16.
7-30 - 8-0 a.m. Squad Drill. Doubling 400 yds.
9-0 a.m. "D" Company - Digging.
9-30 a.m. Remainder of Battalion - Company Training etc. (as on Wednesday) on Cotley Hill.
2-0 p.m. Physical Training - Bayonet Fighting Musketry (Rapid Firing Test).
4-30 p.m. Pay Parade.

SATURDAY 18/3/16.
7-30 - 8-0 a.m. Squad Drill Doubling 400 yds.
9-0 a.m. Physical Training - Bayonet Fighting - Fire Drill.
11-15 a.m. Rifle Inspection by Company Commanders.
11-45 a.m. Interior Economy.

SUNDAY 19/3/16. C H U R C H   P A R A D E.

If the weather on any of the above days is unfavourable for outdoor work, the following programme will be carried out in Barrack Room Huts:-

7-30 - 8-0 a.m. Hut Inspection.
9-30 a.m. - 12-30 p.m. Physical Training, Musketry - Firing Positions, Practice in Muscle Exercises, Rapid Loading, Rapid Aiming & Rapid Firing. Lectures.
2-0 - 5-0 p.m. Bayonet Fighting, Musketry and Lectures.

SUTTON VENY.
11th March 1916.

CAPT. & ADJUTANT.
2/21st Batt. The London R.

Appendix III

2/21st BATTALION, THE LONDON REGIMENT

PROGRAMME OF TRAINING FOR WEEK ENDING 25TH MARCH 1916

220 N.C.Os and men engaged in firing General Musketry Course. Bombers, Signallers & Machine Gun Section follow separate Programmes.

DAILY PROGRAMME - MONDAY to SATURDAY

7-30 - 8-0 a.m.　　　　　　　　"D" Company - Firing.
Squad Drill. Dress :-
Marching Order.　　　　　　　Battalion on Divisional and
　　　　　　　　　　　　　　　Brigade Duties.

SUNDAY

Church Parade.

SUTTON VENY.
18th March 1916.

(signed)
CAPT & ADJUTANT.
2/21st Battalion,
THE LONDON REGIMENT.

Appendroe IV.

2/21st BATTALION, THE LONDON REGIMENT

PROGRAMME OF TRAINING FOR WEEK COMMENCING 27TH MARCH 1916.

MONDAY
27/3/16.   9-0 a.m. Battalion Route March.   2-0 p.m. Physical Training - Bayonet Fighting
                                                                                     and Musketry.

TUESDAY   7-30 - Squad Drill 9-0 a.m. 50 men of "A" Co. Digging.   2-0 p.m. Physical Training -
28/3/16.   8 -0 a.m. & Doubling. 9-30 a.m. Company Training - Artillery Formations -   Bayonet Fighting & Musketry.
                                           Extended Order Drill &c.

WEDNESDAY   7-30 - Squad Drill 9-30 a.m. Company Training - Artillery Formations -   2-0 p.m. Physical Training -
29/3/16.   8 -0 a.m. & Doubling.   Extended Order Drill &c.   Bayonet Fighting - Musketry.

THURSDAY   7-30 - Squad Drill 9-30 a.m. Company Training - Artillery Formations -   2-0 p.m. Physical Training -
30/3/16.   8 -0 a.m. & Doubling.   Extended Order Drill &c.   Bayonet Fighting - Musketry.
                                 1-30 p.m. 50 men of "B" Co. Digging.   4-30 p.m. Foot Inspection.

FRIDAY   7-30 - Squad Drill 9-30 a.m. Company Training - Artillery Formations -   2-0 p.m. Physical Training -
31/3/16.   8 -0 a.m. & Doubling.   Extended Order Drill &c.   Bayonet Fighting - Musketry.
                                 1-30 p.m. 50 men of "C" Co. Digging.   4-30 p.m. Pay Parade.

SATURDAY   7-30 a.m. Squad Drill 9 -0 a.m. Physical Training - Bayonet Fighting - Fire Drill.
1/4/16.   8 -0 a.m. & Doubling.11-15 a.m. Rifle Inspection by Company Commanders.
                                 11-45 p.m. Interior Economy.

SUNDAY 2/4/16   C H U R C H   P A R A D E

If weather on any of the above days is unfavourable for outdoor work, the following Programme will be carried out in Barrack Room Huts :-

7-30 - 8-0 a.m.   2-0 - 5-0 p.m.
Hut Inspection.   Physical Training - Musketry - Firing Positions, Practice in   Bayonet Fighting - Musketry
                   Muscle Exercises. Rapid Loading, Rapid Aiming & Rapid Firing.   and Lectures.

SUTTON VENY.
                                                                    [signature]
27th March 1916.   CAPT. & ADJUTANT.
                                                                    2/21st Battalion,
                                                                    THE LONDON REGIMENT.

Vol. 2 No. 4.

War Diary
of the
2/21st Battalion, Lond. Regt.
from
1st to 30th April 1916.

Confidential

WAR DIARY
or
INTELLIGENCE SUMMARY.

(Erase heading not required.) Ref. Ord Sheet 282 1"to 1 mile

Army Form C. 2118.

Place	Date	Hour	Summary of Events and Information	Remarks and references to Appendices
SUTTON VENY	April 1	7.30	General Training in Camp.	
"	" 2		Church Parade	
"	" 3	7.30	General Training see Appendix 1	Appendix I
"	" 4		24 sets Officers equipment received	
"	" 5		"Alarm" sounded for practice at 4.2 p.m. Signallers Telescope received	
"	" 6			
"	" 7		General Training see Appendix I	
"	" 8			
"	" 9			
"	" 10		16 Trench Shelters received	
"	" 11		25 Mag: Compasses received	
"	" 12			
"	" 13		General Training see Appendix II	16 Binoculars Pris. received
"	" 14			6 Wagons Limber G.S. received
"	" 15			777,000 rounds Mark VII received
"	" 16			"Alarm" sounded for practice at 9.0 a.m. Appendix II

Army Form C. 2118.

WAR DIARY
or
INTELLIGENCE SUMMARY.
(Erase heading not required.)

Ref. Ord Sheet 287 1" to 1 mile

Instructions regarding War Diaries and Intelligence Summaries are contained in F. S. Regs., Part II. and the Staff Manual respectively. Title pages will be prepared in manuscript.

Place	Date	Hour	Summary of Events and Information	Remarks and references to Appendices
SUTTON VENY	1916 April 14		General Training see Appendix III	Appendix III
	" 15		ditto.	
	" 16		ditto.	
	" 17		ditto.	
	" 18		ditto.	
	" 19		ditto.	
	" 20		ditto.	
	" 21		ditto.	
	" 22		ditto.	
	" 23		ditto.	18 pair Binoculars received
	" 24		General Training see Appendix IV	Appendix IV
	" 25		ditto.	"Alarm" sounded for practice 2.29 p.m.
	" 26		ditto.	
	" 27		ditto.	"Alarm" sounded for practice 4=15 p.m.
	" 28		ditto.	9 Bicycles received
	" 29		ditto.	180 Rifles & 115 Bayonets received
	" 30		ditto.	64,000 rounds Mark VII received
				180 sets Equipment pattern 1914 received

1577 Wt.W10791/1773 500,000 1/15 D. D. & L. A.D.S.S./Forms/C. 2118.

Appendix I

2/21st BATTALION, THE LONDON REGIMENT

PROGRAMME OF TRAINING FOR WEEK COMMENCING .... 3rd APRIL 1916

MONDAY 3/4/16	8-30 a.m.	Route March. 2-0 p.m. Physical Training, Bayonet Fighting & Musketry.
TUESDAY 4/4/16	7-30 - 8-0 a.m.	Squad Drill & Doubling. 9-15 a.m. Battalion Digging. 2-0 p.m. Company Training nr. East Hill Farm. 11-0 a.m. Physical Training & Bayonet Fighting.
WEDNESDAY 5/4/16	7-30 - 8-0 a.m.	Squad Drill & Doubling. 9-30 a.m. Company Training - Artillery Formations 2-0 p.m. Physical Training &c. Extended Order Drill &c. nr. Middle Hill. 8-0 p.m. Battalion Digging.
THURSDAY 6/4/16	7-30 -m 8-0 a.m.	Squad Drill & Doubling. 9-15 a.m. Battalion Digging. 2-0 p.m. Co. Training. East 11-0 a.m. Physical Training & Bayonet Fighting. Hill Farm. 4-30 p.m. Foot Inspection.
FRIDAY 7/4/16	9-0 a.m. 4-30 p.m.	Battalion Outpost Scheme Pay Parade. 8-0 p.m. Battalion Digging.
SATURDAY 8/4/16	7-30 - 8-0 a.m.	Squad Drill & Doubling. 9-0 a.m. Physical Training, Bayonet Fighting, Fire Drill. 11-0 a.m. Interior Economy.

If the weather on any of the above days, is unfavourable for outdoor work, the following programme will be carried out in Barrack Room Huts :-

7-30 - 8-0 a.m. 9-30 a.m. - 12-30 p.m. 2-0 - 5-0 p.m.
Hut Inspection. Physical Training, Musketry - Fire Positions, Practice in Bayonet Fighting, Musketry
  Muscle Exercises, Rapid Loading, Rapid Aiming & Rapid Firing. and Lectures
  Lectures

CAPT. & ADJUTANT.

SUTTON VENY.   2/21st Battalion, The London Regiment.

Appendix II

2/21st BATTALION, THE LONDON REGIMENT

PROGRAMME OF TRAINING FOR WEEK COMMENCING .... 10th APRIL 1916

MONDAY 10/4/16	8-30 a.m.	Route March. 2-0 p.m. "A" Co. Practice over Obstacle Course. Physical Training - Bayonet Fighting - Semaphore Drill.
TUESDAY 11/4/16.	8-45 a.m.	Battalion Digging. 11-0 a.m. Physical Training - Bayonet Fighting 2-0 p.m. Coy. Training nr. North Farm. etc.
WEDNESDAY 12/4/16.	7-30 - 8-0 a.m.	Squad Drill & Doubling. 9-30 a.m. Company Training etc. on 2-0 p.m. Physical Training - Bayonet area nr. Middle Hill. Fighting etc. "C" Co. Practice over Obstacle Course.
THURSDAY 13/4/16.	8-45 a.m.	Battalion Digging. 11-0 a.m. Semaphore Drill. 2-0 p.m. Coy. Training nr. West Hill Farm.
FRIDAY 14/4/16.	9-0 a.m.	Battalion Outpost Scheme. 4-0 p.m. Foot Inspection. 4-30 p.m. Pay Parade. "D" Co. practice over Obstacle Course.
SATURDAY 15/4/16.	7-30 - 8-0 a.m.	Squad Drill & Doubling. 9-0 a.m. Parade under Company arrangements.
SUNDAY 16/4/16		C H U R C H P A R A D E

If the weather on any of the above days is unfavourable for outdoor work, the following Programme will be carried out in Barrack Room Huts :-

7-30 - 8-0 a.m.   9-30 a.m. - 12-30 p.m.   2-0 - 5-0 p.m.
Hut Inspection   Physical Training - Musketry - Firing Positions - Practice in Muscle   Bayonet Fighting - Musketry
                 Exercises, Rapid Loading, Rapid Aiming & Rapid Firing. Lectures.   & Lectures.

The Obstacle Course must only be used at the times shewn.
Men should be trained to send and read semaphore messages.
Digging to be carried out as before. Discipline must be maintained as on service.
Men detailed for firing must do Physical Training every day.

SUTTON VENY 916.
9th April 1916.

Capt. & Adjutant,
2/21st Battalion,
THE LONDON REGIMENT.

Appendix III continued

PROGRAMME OF TRAINING FOR WEEK COMMENCING 17/4/16 (contd)

LECTURES — To all Officers (1) By Staff Captain. On the 18th inst. at 5-0 p.m. in No. 1 Dining Room - "Information obtained during tour in France."
(2) By G.O.C. 60th (London) Division. On the 20th inst. at 5-0 p.m. in Y.M.C.A. Hut, No. 4 Camp.- "Trench Warfare". All Officers, whether on local Courses or on Musketry, must attend the G.O.C's lecture on Thursday at 5-0 p.m.

OBSTACLE COURSE — May be used at other times during the week except on Monday 10 - 11 a.m. & Wednesday 4 - 5 p.m.

WIRE ENTANGLEMENTS — After the Officers and Senior N.C.Os have had a Course of Instruction, they should instruct their Platoons at the earliest opportunity. Companies will parade under their Company Sergeant Majors. When the Officers are on this Course.

INTERIOR ECONOMY — Attention must be paid particularly to waterbottle covers and corks, dirty peaks on caps & long hair.
Attention is again drawn to Battalion Orders of the 10th inst. Men should not be punished for deficiencies in Kit.

NIGHT DIGGING — The same men should/be paraded twice in the same week

DAY DIGGING — Arrangements all as before.

If the weather on any of the above days is unfavourable for outdoor work, the following Programme will be carried out in Barrack Room Huts :-

7-30 - 8-0 a.m.   9-30 a.m. - 12-30 p.m.   2-0 - 5-0 p.m.
Hut Inspection.   Physical Training - Musketry - Firing Positions -   Bayonet Fighting -
                     Practice in Muscle Exercises. Rapid Loading,   Musketry & Lectures.
                     Rapid Aiming & Rapid Firing. Lectures

SUTTON VENY.
16th April 1916.

CAPT. & ADJUTANT.
2/21st Battalion,
THE LONDON REGIMENT.

Appendix IV

2/21st. Battalion The London Regiment

PROGRAMME OF TRAINING FOR WEEK COMMENCING...24/4/16.

Monday 24/4/16	7-0- 7-45am.	Drill Parade	8-30am. Battalion Route March	4-0pm. Foot Inspection.
Tuesday 25/4/16	7-0- 7-45am.	Drill Parade	9-0am. Company Training on Area nr. Cotley Hill.	2-0pm. Coy.Training in Camp "B" Co.Obstacle Course	8-0pm.Battalion Dig by night.
Wednesday 26/4/16	7-0- 7-45am.	Drill Parade	9-0am. Battalion Parade for B± Digging	2-0pm. Coy.Training On Area nr. Middle Hill.
Thursday 27/4/16	7-0- 7-45am.	Drill Parade	9-0am. Company Training - Fire Discipline.	3-30pm.Lecture - "Trench Warfare."
Friday 28/4/16	7-0- 7-45am.	Drill Parade	9-0am. Battalion Training in Attack	3-30pm.Lecture - Discipline. Army Act to be read.
Saturday 29/4/16	7-0- 7-45am.	Drill Parade	9-0am. Parade under Coy Arrangements-Interior Economy	11-0am."A" Coy. Obstacle Course.
Sunday 30/4/16			C H U R C H P A R A D E.	

If the weather on any of the above days is unfavourable for outdoor work, the following Programme will be carried out in Barracks Room Huts:-

7-30 - 8-0am.   9-30am. - 12-30pm.   2-0 - 5-0pm.
Hut Inspection   Physical Training - Musketry - Firing Positions - Practice in Muscle   Bayonet Fighting -
                  Exercises,Rapid Loading,Rapid Aiming, & Rapid Firing. Lectures.   Musketry & Lectures.

CAPT. & ADJUTANT
2/21st Battalion,
THE LONDON REGIMENT.

Sutton Veny
23/4/16

Vol 2 No 5

Confidential

War Diary
of the
2/21st Battalion London Regiment
from
1st to 31st May 1916.

Army Form C. 2118.

WAR DIARY
or
INTELLIGENCE SUMMARY.
(Erase heading not required.)

Ref. Ord Sheet 57 1" to 1 mile

Place	Date	Hour	Summary of Events and Information	Remarks and references to Appendices
SITTEN VENY	1916			
	Aug 1/4		Training as per Weekly Programme	see Appendix I — App. I
"	6/14		Training as per Weekly Programme	see Appendix II — App. II
"	10		Bottles Water received 19 x	
"	15/21		Training as per Weekly Programme	see Appendix III — App. III
"	22/28		ditto	see Appendix IV — " IV
"	29/31		ditto	see Appendix V — " V
"	30		Sets of Patt 1914 Equipment received 985.	

Signed,
Capt. + Adj.
7/1st Batt. Kn. Regt.

Army Form C. 2118.

WAR DIARY
or
INTELLIGENCE SUMMARY.

(Erase heading not required.)

Instructions regarding War Diaries and Intelligence Summaries are contained in F. S. Regs., Part II. and the Staff Manual respectively. Title pages will be prepared in manuscript.

Place	Date	Hour	Summary of Events and Information	Remarks and references to Appendices

1577 Wt.W10791/1773 500,000 1/15 D. D. & L. A.D.S.S./Forms/C. 2118.

Appendix I

2/21st BATTALION THE LONDON REGIMENT.

PROGRAMME OF TRAINING FOR WEEK COMMENCING............1ST MAY 1916.

MONDAY 1/5/16	7-0 - 7-45am.	Drill Parade	9-0am. "C" Coy. Obstacle Course and Bayonet Fighting 9-0am. 3 Companies Digging. 11-30am. Parade under Company Arrangements. 2-0pm. Company Training in Camp, "B" Coy. Obstacle Course.
TUESDAY 2/5/16	7-0 - 7-45am.	Drill Parade	9-0am. Battalion Training under C.O. 4-0pm. Foot Inspection.
WEDNESDAY 3/5/16	7-0 - 7-45am.	Drill Parade	9-0am Brigade Route March. 8-0pm. 2 Companies Night Digging.
THURSDAY 4/5/16	7-0 - 7-45am.	Drill Parade	TRENCH SCHEME UNDER BRIGADE ARRANGEMENTS
FRIDAY 5/5/16	7-0 - 7-45am.	Drill Parade	9-0am. Battalion Training under C.O. 8-0pm. Battalion Night March.
SATURDAY 6/5/16	7-0 - 7-45am.	Drill Parade	9-0am Parade under Company Arrangements - Interior Economy. "D" Company Obstacle Course.
SUNDAY 7/5/16			C H U R C H P A R A D E

Gas Helmets for Instruction will be drawn from Q.M. Stores. Tuesday "C" Co. Wednesday "B" Co.
Thursday "D" Co. Saturday "A" Co.
Company Commanders will arrange that Company Bombers will have practice in throwing the dummy bombs.

SUTTON VENY
30/4/16

[signature]
CAPTAIN & ADJUTANT.
2/21st Battalion,The London Regt.

Appendix II

2/21st BATTALION, THE LONDON REGIMENT.

SCHEDULE OF TRAINING FOR WEEK COMMENCING 8th MAY 1916.

MONDAY 8/5/16.	7 - 8 Drill Parade. 7-45 a.m.	8-9 a.m. Company training on area nr. Middle Hill. 2-4 p.m. Company Training in Camp. - Bayonet fighting & Obstacle Course.	6-9 p.m. Night digging.
TUESDAY 9/5/16		9-0 a.m. Battalion training under C.O.	4-5 p.m. Obstacle Course.
WEDNESDAY 10/5/16.	7 - 8 Drill 7-45 a.m. Parade.	9-0 a.m. Brigade route march.	4-5 p.m. Foot Inspection.
THURSDAY 11/5/16.		8-45 a.m. Battalion digging. 11-30 a.m. Parade under Company arrangements.	2-5 p.m. Coy. Training - Fire Discipline - Bayonet fighting - Obstacle Course.
FRIDAY 12/5/16	7 - 8 Drill 7-45 a.m. Parade.	TRENCH ATTACK UNDER BRIGADE ARRANGEMENTS.	
SATURDAY 13/5/16.	7 - 8 Drill 7-45 a.m. Parade.	9-0 a.m. Parade under Coy. arrangements - Interior Economy - Obstacle Course.	
SUNDAY 14/5/16.		C H U R C H P A R A D E S	

Company Commanders must give as much time as possible during the week to BAYONET FIGHTING.

(signed) Greenall

CAPT. & ADJUTANT.
2/21st Battalion.
THE LONDON REGIMENT.

UPTON V MN.
7th May 1916.

Appendix III

2/5th BATTALION. THE LONDON REGIMENT

PROGRAMME OF TRAINING FOR WEEK COMMENCING 15/5/16

(BATTALION OF DIVISIONAL & BRIGADE DUTIES)

MONDAY 15/5/16	7 – 8 Drill Parade. 7–45 a.m.	8–30 a.m. – 10–30 a.m. – N.C.Os & Officers, N.C.Os & men for Coy. Fire Management Instruction. 9 –0 a.m. Coy. Training in Camp – Physical Training – Bayonet fighting, etc. 2–2 p.m. Company Training.
TUESDAY 16/5/16	7 – 8 Drill Parade. 7–45 a.m.	9 –0 a.m. Company Training, with Field Cooking. 2–0 P.m. Coy. Training – Fire Discipline – Bayonet fighting. 3.30 P.m. – 12.30 a.m. – N Officers, N.C.Os and men per Company. Fire Management Instruction.
WEDNESDAY 17/5/16	7 – 8 Drill Parade. 7–45 a.m.	9 –0 a.m. Coy. Training in Camp. Physical Training – Bayonet fighting – Chapel's Course. 2 –0 P.m. Coy. Training.
THURSDAY 18/5/16	7 – 8 Drill Parade. 7–45 a.m.	9 –0 a.m. Battalion Training under C.O. 4 –0 P.m. Foot Inspection.
FRIDAY 19/5/16	7 – 8 Drill Parade. 7–45 a.m.	BRIGADE TRAINING.
SATURDAY 20/5/16	7 – 8 Drill Parade. 7–45 a.m.	9 –8 a.m. Parade under Co. Arrangements – Interior Economy etc.
SUNDAY 21/5/16		CHURCH PARADE.

Officers, Sgts. Sgt. Major. and Drums Majors will fire a Revolver Course during the week.

SUTTON VENY.
13th May 1916.

[signature]
CAPT. & ADJUTANT.
2/5th Battalion,
THE LONDON REGIMENT.

Appendix IV

2/21st BATTALION, THE LONDON REGIMENT.

PROGRAMME OF TRAINING FOR WEEK COMMENCING 22nd MAY 1916.

MONDAY 22/5/16	7-0 – 7-45 a.m. Drill Parade.	9-0 a.m. Battalion Instruction in Trench Routine & Headline – Sutton Veny Trenches.
TUESDAY 23/5/16	7-0 – 7-45 a.m. Drill Parade.	9-0 a.m. Company Training. 2-0 p.m. Company Training. – Bayonet Fighting – Physical Training – Box Instruction.
WEDNESDAY 24/5/16		DIVISIONAL ROUTE MARCH
THURSDAY 25/5/16		BRIGADE ATTACK
FRIDAY 26/5/16		DIVISIONAL ATTACK
SATURDAY 27/5/16		9-0 a.m. March under Company arrangements – Interior Economy – Bayonet Fighting – Chuhole Board.
SUNDAY 28/5/16		CHURCH PARADE.

SUTTON VENY
21st May 1916.

(signed)
Capt. & ADJUTANT.
2/21st Battalion,
The LONDON REGIMENT.

Appendix V.

2/21st BATTALION. THE LONDON REGT.

PROGRAMME OF TRAINING FOR THE WEEK COMMENCING 29th MAY 1916

MONDAY 29/5/16	7-0a.m.	A & D Coy. Field Firing. B-Coy. C & D Coy. Parade for Coy. Training. B-Coys. A & B Coys. Bayonet Fighting & Obstacle Course.
TUESDAY 30/5/16	7-0 – 7-45a.m.	Drill Parade. 8-0 a.m. C & D Coy. Parade for Bayonet Fighting & Physical Training
WEDNESDAY 31/5/16		BATTALION UNDER COMMANDING OFFICER ROYAL REVIEW
THURSDAY 1/6/16	7-0 – 7-45a.m.	Drill Parade. 8-Coy.a.m. C & D Coys. Parade for Bayonet Fighting Bomb Throwing etc. 8-Coy.m. A & B Coys. Field Firing. 8-Coys. A & B Coys. Parade for Coy. Training
FRIDAY 2/6/16	7-0 – 7-45a.m.	Drill Parade. 8-0a.m. BATTALION TRAINING
SATURDAY 3/6/16	7-0 – 7-45a.m.	Drill Parade. 8-0a.m. Interior Economy
SUNDAY 4/6/16		CHURCH PARADE

SIGNED A.E.WAY
27th May 1916

(signature)
MAJOR & ADJUTANT
2/ 1st Battalion
THE LONDON REGT.

www.ingramcontent.com/pod-product-compliance
Lightning Source LLC
Chambersburg PA
CBHW081424160426
43193CB00013B/2188